PRAISE FOR *Conversations with Scripture: Revelation*

"For many years now church leaders have been complaining that the biblical literacy of most denominations is falling. While that fact is not in dispute, what to do about it is a perennial debate. Now we may have an answer. *Conversations with Scripture* is a new series that is accessible, well written and intelligent. If we need to help people open the Bible, this series one of the most effective efforts we have made in a generation." —The Rt. Rev. Steven Charleston, President and Dean of the Episcopal Divinity School

"An exciting new resource in the area of Adult Christian Formation, Frederick W. Schmidt's *Revelation* is smart and accessible. The sidebar definitions, suggested resources and accompanying study questions provide clear guideposts into the not often entered world of apocalyptic literature. With a keen sense of Anglican theological heritage, Schmidt creates a welcome mat and friendly companion on the road to a more intimate knowledge of God's revelation through scripture." —The Rev. Canon Anne E. Kitch, Canon for Christian Formation at the Cathedral Church of the Nativity in the Diocese of Bethlehem and author of *The Anglican Family Prayer Book*

CONVERSATIONS
WITH SCRIPTURE:
REVELATION

CONVERSATIONS
WITH SCRIPTURE:

REVELATION

FREDERICK W. SCHMIDT

morehouse

HARRISBURG • LONDON

Morehouse Publishing and the Anglican Association of Biblical Scholars thank the Louisville Institute for their interest in and support of this series.

Morehouse Publishing, P.O. Box 1321, Harrisburg, PA 17105

Morehouse Publishing, The Tower Building, 11 York Road, London SE1 7NX

Morehouse Publishing is a Continuum imprint.

Cover art: Limbourg Brothers (15th century CE). *Saint John on Patmos.* Illuminated miniature from the Très Riches Heures du Duc de Berry. 1416. Courtesy of Réunion des Musées Nationaux / Art Resource, NY.

Cover design by Corey Kent

Series design by Beth Oberholtzer

Library of Congress Cataloging-in-Publication Data

Schmidt, Frederick W.
    Conversations with Scripture : Revelation / by Frederick W. Schmidt.
       p.   cm. — (Anglican Association of Biblical Scholars study series)
    Includes bibliographical references.
    ISBN 0-8192-2107-4 (pbk.)
    1. Bible. N.T. Revelation—Criticism, interpretation, etc.   I. Title.
II. Series.
BS2825.52.S36   2005
228'.06—dc22

                                      2004019288

Printed in the United States of America

05 06 07 08 09   10 9 8 7 6 5 4 3 2 1

For Douglas "Jake" Jacobsen, David John Schlafer,
and William Vance Trollinger Jr.

As Cicero observed, when asked about the gift of friendship,
"What can be more delightful than to have
some one to whom you can say everything
with the same absolute confidence as to yourself?"

Gracious God, grant us the faith, courage, strength, and hope of your servant John: That we might discern the true nature of the present and the difference between the cities of our making and yours. For the sake of your Son, our Savior, Jesus Christ, who lives and reigns with you and the Holy Spirit, one God, now and forever.

AMEN.

Blessed Lord, who caused all holy Scriptures to be written for our learning: Grant us so to hear them, read, mark, learn, and inwardly digest them, that we may embrace and ever hold fast the blessed hope of everlasting life, which you have given us in our Savior Jesus Christ; who lives and reigns with you and the Holy Spirit, one God, for ever and ever.

AMEN.

CONTENTS

INTRODUCTION
TO THE SERIES

To talk about a distinctively Anglican approach to Scripture is a daunting task. Within any one part of the larger church that we call the Anglican Communion there is, on historical grounds alone, an enormous variety. But as the global character of the church becomes apparent in ever-newer ways, the task of accounting for that variety, while naming the characteristics of a distinctive approach, becomes increasingly difficult.

In addition, the examination of Scripture is not confined to formal studies of the kind addressed in this series of parish studies written by formally trained biblical scholars. Systematic theologian David Ford, who participated in the 1998 Lambeth Conference, rightly noted that although "most of us have studied the Bible over many years" and "are aware of various academic approaches to it," we have "also lived in it" and "inhabited it, through worship, preaching, teaching and meditation." As such, Ford observes, "The Bible in the Church is like a city we have lived in for a long time." We may not be able to account for the history of every building or the architecture on every street, but we know our way around and it is a source of life to each of us.[1]

That said, we have not done as much as we should in acquainting the inhabitants of that famed city with the architecture that lies within. So, as risky as it may seem, it is important to describe the sights and sounds of the city we call the Bible that matter most to its Anglican residents.

The first of those descriptors that leaps to mind is familiar, basic, and forever debated: *authoritative.* Years ago I was asked by a colleague who belonged to the Evangelical Free Church why someone with as much obvious interest in the Bible would be an Episcopal priest. I responded, "Because we read the whole of Scripture and not just the parts of it that suit us." Scripture has been and continues to play a singular role in the life of the Anglican Communion, but it has rarely been used in the sharply prescriptive fashion that has characterized some traditions.

Some have characterized this approach as an attempt to navigate a *via media* between overbearing control and an absence of accountability. But I think it is far more helpful to describe the tensions not as a matter of steering a course between two different and competing priorities, but as the complex dance necessary to live under a very different, but typically Anglican notion of authority itself. Authority shares the same root as the word "to author" and as such, refers first and foremost, not to the *power* to *control* with all that both of those words suggest, but to the capacity to *author creativity*, with all that both of those words suggest.[2] As such, the function of Scripture is to carve out a creative space in which the work of the Holy Spirit can yield the very kind of fruit associated with its work in the church. The difficulty, of course, is that for that space to be creative, it is also necessary for it to have boundaries, much like the boundaries we establish for other kinds of genuinely creative freedom: the practice of scales for concert pianists, the discipline of work at the barre that frees the ballerina, or the guidance that parents provide for their children. Defined in this way, it is possible to see the boundaries around that creative space as barriers to be eliminated, or as walls that provide protection, but they are neither.

And so the struggle continues with the authority of Scripture. From time to time in the Anglican Communion, it has been and will be treated as a wall that protects us from the complexity of navigating without error the world in which we live. At other times, it will be treated as the ancient remains of a city to be cleared away in favor of a brave new world. But both approaches are rooted, not in the limitations of Scripture, but in our failure to welcome the creative space we have been given.

For that reason, at their best, Anglican approaches to Scripture are also *illuminative*. William Sloane Coffin once observed that the problem with Americans and the Bible is that we read it like a drunk uses a lamppost. We lean on it, we don't use it for illumination.[3] Leaning on Scripture and having the lamppost taken out completely are simply two very closely related ways of failing to acknowledge the creative space provided by Scripture. But once the creative space is recognized for what it is, then the importance of reading Scripture for illumination becomes apparent. Application of the insight Scripture provides into who we are and what we might become is not something that can be prescribed or mapped out in detail. It is only a conversation with Scripture, marked by humility, that can begin to spell out the particulars. Reading Scripture is, then, in the Anglican tradition a delicate and demanding task, that involves both the careful listening for the voice of God and courageous conversation with the world around us.

It is, for that reason, an approach that is also marked by *critical engagement* with the text itself. It is no accident that from 1860 to 1900 the three best-known names in the world of biblical scholarship were Anglican priests, the first two of whom were bishops: B. F. Westcott, J. B. Lightfoot, and F. J. A. Hort. Together the three made contributions to both the church and the critical study of the biblical text that became a defining characteristic of Anglican life.

Of the three, Westcott's contribution, perhaps, best captures the balance. Not only did his work contribute to a critical text of the Greek New Testament that would eventually serve as the basis for the English Revised Version, but as Bishop of Durham he also convened a conference of Christians to discuss the arms race in Europe, founded the Christian Social Union, and mediated the Durham coal strike of 1892.

The English roots of the tradition are not the only, or even the defining, characteristic of Anglican approaches to Scripture. The church, no less than the rest of the world, has been forever changed by the process of globalization, which has yielded a rich *diversity* that complements the traditions once identified with the church.

Scripture in Uganda, for example, has been read with an emphasis on private, allegorical, and revivalist applications. The result has been a tradition in large parts of East Africa that stresses the reading of Scripture on one's own: the direct application made to the contemporary situation without reference to the setting of the original text; and the combination of personal testimony with the power of public exhortation.

At the same time, however, globalization has brought that tradition into conversation with people from other parts of the Anglican Communion, as the church in Uganda has sought to bring the biblical text to bear on its efforts to address the issues of justice, poverty, war, disease, food shortage, and education. In such a dynamic environment, the only thing that one can say with certainty is that neither the Anglican Communion, nor the churches of East Africa, will ever be the same again.

Authoritative, illuminative, critical, and varied—these are not the labels that one uses to carve out an approach to Scripture that can be predicted with any kind of certainty. Indeed, if the word *dynamic* is added to the list, perhaps all that one can predict is still more change! But such is the nature of life in any city, including one shaped by the Bible. We influence the shape of its life, but we are also shaped and nurtured by it. And if that city is of God's making, then to force our own design on the streets and buildings around us is to disregard the design that the chief architect has in mind.

—Frederick W. Schmidt
Series Editor

AUTOBIOGRAPHICAL
NOTE

A theological education can be a bit like assembling a child's toy on Christmas Eve. Lots of pieces, no idea how they fit together. Biblical interpretation and systematic theology are just two of the pieces strewn across the floor. Years ago when I worked on a masters of divinity, the people who helped me get the pieces out of the box were loath to help me put them together.

Biblical scholars were quick to expose me to the complexities of the text: opaque images, allusive words, debatable grammar, history that was difficult to reconstruct. Pieces within pieces. The professors who taught me how to interpret Scripture had a gift for surfacing the complexity and the clearly human character of the text, but they were hard-pressed to tell me how it could be authoritative for someone living over two millennia later.

Systematic theologians had a different box of pieces. Gifted at outlining what should be believed in an ordered fashion, the Bible's authority was central to much of what they taught. But they were no more willing to help me grapple with the complex character of the text than the biblical scholars were willing to deal with questions of scriptural authority.

I am an Anglican today, in part, because (in theory, at any rate) our approach to theological formulation requires an answer to both questions. We are sufficiently grounded in the realities of the text—devoted, if you will, to taking the Bible as we find it—so that we are unwilling to shy away from dealing with the challenges that we find there. We know the Bible was shaped by the language, culture, and issues of worlds that no longer exist as such. But we also hold that

Scripture has a generative place of privilege in our history as a community of faith that defines what we must be, if we are to call ourselves Christians.

Just how that complex process of putting together the pieces of Scripture, tradition, and reason that we have accumulated in over two millennia is accomplished goes well beyond the boundaries of this brief, autobiographical note. The floor is now littered with those pieces. Indeed, I sometimes wonder whether the complexity of the task is one that Anglicans of every stripe find so daunting that they are willing to give their children the pieces largely unassembled. Watching our small part of the Anglican Communion in action recently, a Lutheran friend observed, "You Episcopalians certainly seem to talk a lot about what you feel and what you've experienced, but you don't talk about theology very much." And I am afraid that he is right.

But if that is so, it is a departure from a heritage that once consecrated scholars as bishops and combined theological depth with a passion for engagement with the world. It is that task which prompted me to become an Anglican and it continues to shape my work. This brief introduction to John's Apocalypse is part of that effort. I am convinced that as Anglicans, this part of Scripture is one that needs to be reclaimed for our tradition. Misread, misunderstood, and often neglected, it presents us with the challenge of reading Scripture with our eyes wide open, but it also has much to say to our lives.

INTRODUCTION

When I was young, visits to my cousins' home included long, late hours reading comic books and discussing the fantastic predictions of Edgar Cacye. Reputed to be one of history's true clairvoyants, Cacye is hailed by a small, but enduring circle of readers as someone who successfully predicted events far ahead of his time. The fall of communism, dramatic climactic changes, and a shift in the earth's poles are all cited as examples of Cacye's psychic powers.

Fascination with predictions of this kind has been a recurring feature of religious life in the United States, but such predictions are hardly unique to the American spiritual landscape. Given that fascination, it is not surprising that the Bible's Book of Revelation (or what is sometimes called "John's Apocalypse" or "the Apocalypse") has been and is a seedbed of equally speculative prophecies. Filled with images and vignettes that range from the obscure to the bizarre, John's Apocalypse invites guesses about the book's meaning and the significance of individual passages. In response, interpreters have been quick to satisfy that curiosity. With one eye on the details of the text and another eye on the crises erupting around the world, they have made suggestion after suggestion about the connections between the words of Revelation and the events of history past, present, and future.

As a result, everywhere you turn today, if people read the Book of Revelation at all, they read it with this Bible-as-roadmap-to-the-future view. Over the years that approach has, in turn, spawned a left-behind spirituality and theology, lending still more apparent authority to the approach. Preoccupied with who will and who will not be delivered in "the last days," someone has to be "left behind," if others are to move into heaven.

The impact of this approach has been widespread. Years ago, when I was teaching undergraduates on a regular basis, I often surveyed incoming freshmen. One of the more open-ended questions that I asked invited students to identify the one thing about the Bible they wanted to know more about. There was always a rich variety of suggestions, but time and again, the Book of Revelation surfaced as a topic of interest. Some wanted to know, "When is the end coming?" Others wanted to know, "Who is the Antichrist?"

Such questions continue unabated. At the time of writing this book, the fictional *Left Behind* series written by Tim LaHaye and Jerry Jenkins, which explores one possible way in which the final days might unravel, continues to sell in record-breaking numbers. And the authors themselves argue that apart from the question of precise detail, theirs is an accurate rendering of Revelation's meaning.

Other students admitted to a generalized anxiety about the content of John's Apocalypse or said that what they had heard about it kept them from reading it at all. But what became clear was that most of the students, regardless of their religious training, assumed that the roadmap approach to the Book of Revelation was the one and only legitimate way to read it.

That, however, is quite simply not the case and in fact, the approach used by LaHaye and others is arguably all but completely foreign to Anglican readings of Scripture. Toward that end, in the pages that follow I will examine the "left-behind" approach and offer an alternative to reading the Book of Revelation in simple, straightforward terms. In what follows you will find:

- An introduction to the three dominant approaches to the Book of Revelation
- An evaluation of each approach
- An illustration of how one of those approaches in particular makes sense of the book
- And a description of the spiritual and theological issues at stake

What I hope you will take away from your reading is this: confidence that there are different ways of reading the Book of Revelation; an awareness of the difference those approaches make to your understanding of the book; and insight into the very real differences those approaches make to your life both spiritually and theologically.

 # Revelation as Roadmap

In the wake of the events in New York and Washington, D.C., on September 11, 2001, the phone in my department of the seminary where I work began ringing. One of the first calls was from a reporter who asked the question that everyone wanted to ask: "Is what happened today a sign of the end?" That question provides a clue to the most popular way of reading the Book of Revelation; many people read it as a roadmap. Widely popular—even in circles where people avoid reading John's Apocalypse—it enjoys the presumption of being the right way to read this difficult book. People may or may not embrace it, but even those who don't often assume that if you are going to read the Book of Revelation, this is the way it must be read.

I refer to this approach as roadmap-reading because those who interpret Revelation and other parts of Scripture in this fashion use it like a roadmap to the future. In it they find a blow-by-blow description of earth's final days, the judgment of all humankind, and the transformation of heaven and earth. Matching images with events, the reader is able to determine which of the events described there have transpired. If some of them have, then the reader has a rough idea of what will happen next. If some have not, then the reader enjoys the reassurance that they will happen—and soon. They have a map. They know what lies ahead.

There are other labels that I could have used. Some use the word *millennialist* or *chiliast*, both of which refer to a thousand-year reign of peace on earth under Christ's leadership, found in Rev 20:4–6f.

Others use the word *dispensationalist*, which refers to the notion that history, including the end-times, is divided into "eras" during which God acts in distinctive ways. Apart from their obscurity, the problem with these labels is that each of them draws on specific motifs in John's Apocalypse or refers to just one expression of roadmap-reading. So I hope that the label "roadmap" will provide a means of capturing the inspiration of this approach that is both memorable and descriptive.

> The revelation of Jesus Christ, which God gave him to show his servants what must soon take place; he made it known by sending his angel to his servant John . . . —REV 1:1

Given the nature of roadmap-readings, it is easy to get lost in a conversation about what may or may not be a "sign" and about how those signs line up with the language of John's Apocalypse. Such conversations inevitably flounder on intractable debates about the significance of some of the more obscure images that the writer uses and questions about the way those images relate to events in the world around us. That said, most if not all of the interpretations that take this approach make many of the same assumptions about this extraordinary part of the Greek Testament.

Assumptions

One assumption is that John's visions describe events that await conclusion in the near—read, "our"—future. The opening line of the Apocalypse is taken literally and personally: "The revelation of Jesus Christ, which God gave him to show his servants what *must soon take place*" (Rev 1:1; emphasis mine). For that reason, the history of this interpretive approach is marked by a tendency to invent and reinvent the connections between the book and each generation's historical experience.

At the turn of the first century, for example, widespread speculation connected the visions of Revelation with the collapse of the Roman Empire and the repeated invasions that ravaged Rome. Historians of the period recorded that people so feared the coming judgment that they cried "tears of repentance" until "the tears ran down their legs, even to their toes."[1] While refusing to comment directly on the book, centuries later Martin Luther, the great Protestant reformer, included block prints in his translation of Scripture that portrayed

The history of this interpretive approach is marked by a tendency to invent and reinvent the connections between the book and each generation's historical experience.

the whore of Babylon (Rev 17:3f.) as a figure wearing a papal tiara. Since then Protestants have, from time to time, identified one pope or another with the Antichrist and in the early 1960s some American Protestants even ventured an identification of Catholic president John Fitzgerald Kennedy with the infamous 666.

Such identifications are not unique to Protestantism, however. Nor can they be isolated to a single culture. A similar roadmap-reading of Christian traditions prompted Russian poet and publicist Valerii Khatiushin to argue that the disintegration of the Soviet Union was the work of Satan and to predict that Russia would reemerge, Christlike, as the leader of the world in the year 2000.

This sense of a specific connection with each generation's experience is closely tied to a second characteristic of roadmap interpretations that sees the events described in the Book of Revelation and other passages of Scripture as part of a timetable. There is considerable difference of opinion among its proponents about the precise sequence of events. Some believe, for example, that Christ will return before the millennium, or a thousand years of peace (premillennialists). Others believe that the return of Christ will follow it (post-millennialists). And still others believe that the so-called reign of Christ will be a reign manifested in the hearts of those who are faithful (a-millennialists).

Pre-millennialists: those who believe that Christ will return before the millennium (or a thousand years of peace)

Post-millennialists: those who believe that Christ will return after the millennium

A-millennialists: those who believe that the so-called reign of Christ will be manifested in the hearts of those who are faithful

Roadmap-readings of Revelation also differ on the timing of the "rapture": a taking up of the faithful with Christ, while others are "left behind" to face the final judgment of God. Some believe that the rapture will happen before a time of tribulation or trial mentioned in Revelation (pre-tribulationists). Others believe it will happen after the tribulation (post-tribulationists), and still others believe it will happen in the midst of that experience (mid-tribulationists).

The result is a complex series of variations. But the broad sequence of events remains largely the same:

- The moral decline of civilization
- The rise of the Antichrist
- A reign of terror or great tribulation
- The Battle of Armageddon in which the Antichrist is defeated
- The establishment of a thousand year's reign
- A final revolt by Satan that is easily countered
- The resurrection of the dead
- The final judgment
- The creation of a new heaven and a new earth

As such, another characteristic of most roadmap-readings is the interpreter's ability to locate himself or herself in relationship to those events. Those who read the Book of Revelation in this fashion vary in the way that they approach this task. For much of history, those roadmap-readings often located the interpreter somewhere in the midst of those events. Those who do are called "historicists." They can look back at events, decide which ones in the biblical timetable have occurred and, on that basis, project which ones are yet to happen.

But of late, interpreters have more often thought of themselves as living on the cusp of those events. Known as "futurists," these interpreters believe that the events described in the Book of Revelation have yet to occur. This does not mean, however, that the futurists lack an interest in current events. Believing themselves to be living on the "last days," they focus on signs that the end is near. In a widely publicized story, for example, President Ronald Reagan is said to have speculated that an imminent nuclear war with the Soviet Union might, in fact, be God's way of bringing Armageddon to the earth as described in Rev 16:16.

President Ronald Reagan is said to have speculated that an imminent nuclear war with the Soviet Union might, in fact, be God's way of bringing Armageddon to the earth as described in Rev 16:16.

Predictions of this kind, of course, assume that the images used in John's Apocalypse are of a literal character and can be unpacked in a one-to-one correspondence with real people, places, and events. So, those who rely upon a roadmap-reading of Revelation are not just relying upon certain kinds of assumptions about the focus of John's vision, but about the nature of the literature itself. For this reason, the process of interpretation is far more akin to decoding the book than it is to interpretation. Attempting to pique his readers' interest, Hal Lindsey, one of the late-twentieth-century's leading roadmap-readers declared:

> The Bible predicted certain signs which were to herald man's dooms-day. Over the past 20 years, world developments have fulfilled prophe-cies set forth by seers in both the Old and New Testaments. These include: the rebirth of Israel, an increase in natural catastrophes, the threat of war with Egypt and the revival of interest in Satanism and witchcraft. All these happenings were foreseen by prophets from Moses to Jesus as being the key signals for the coming of an Antichrist. And a war which will bring man to the brink of destruction . . . [2]

Real people, real places, and real events—all con-temporary with his readers—are at the front of Lindsey's approach.

These are demonic spirits . . . who go abroad to the kings of the whole world. . . . And they assembled them at the place that in Hebrew is called Armagedon. —REV 16:14, 16

If it seems strange to interpret a biblical text in this way, it may be because the still deeper assumptions that make this kind of approach pos-sible are all but invisible and touch not just upon the Book of Revelation, but also upon the nature of God and the Bible itself. Set out in almost propositional form, those deeper assumptions are these:

- God can do what God wants to do.
- From God's mouth to our ear, Scripture describes what God plans to do.
- Those who take God's plan seriously take Scripture seriously.
- To take Scripture seriously means taking propositions one and two at face value.

In tandem with the assumptions the roadmap-reading makes about the nature of John's Apocalypse, the interpretation has a cer-tain air of inevitability about it. But for those who interpret the book this way, it also carries with it a sense of moral responsibility. Interviewed about the last of his *Left Behind* novels, retired minister Tim LaHaye observed that most people "'don't take the Bible literally. They categorize and mythologize it and read into it their own preconceived ideas. They don't think a loving God will send people to hell.' He will."[3]

Back to the Future

Roadmap-readings of the Church's life are older than the Book of Revelation itself. There is evidence, for example, in the Epistle to the Thessalonians that many in the early church expected the quick return of Christ and the end of all things. Reading between the lines, the Thessalonians believed that these events were so imminent that no one in the community of faith would die before Christ returned. When, in the natural course of things, members of the church did die, members who were distressed by these developments expressed their concern. In response, Paul wrote back, reassuring the Thessalonians that their part in the resurrection was so certain, that even those who were still alive would not precede the "dead in Christ" (1 Thess 4:16).

Similarly, after the destruction of the Temple in 70 CE, the members of Mark's church seem to have concluded that the end was near. Evidence of this expectation appears in chapter 13. There the evangelist uses scattered sayings of Jesus in a larger speech of his own that addresses this issue. Evidently concerned that his church was increasingly distracted by a fascination with those signs, the evangelist mentions a number of them, including the destruction of the Temple. But Mark's Jesus does not encourage the people to pay particular attention to those events. Instead, using the words of Jesus, he repeatedly tells them, "be alert," "keep alert," "keep awake" (Mark 13:23, 33, 37).

Roadmap-readings are older than the Book of Revelation itself. There is evidence in the Epistle to the Thessalonians that many in the early church expected the quick return of Christ and the end of all things.

Although its popularity varied, roadmap-readings of the future continued to surface from time to time in the life of the church. Inspired both by John's Apocalypse and by the images and ideas that surface there, significant individuals and groups took this approach. In 156 CE, Montanus, who lived in Phrygia, assembled a group of followers. Declaring himself the "Spirit of Truth," he presented himself as a guide to the future. His followers, caught up in the emotions of the moment, claimed to see the New Jerusalem descending from heaven. With what they felt sure was the end of all things at hand, they lived lives marked by extreme abstinence. In spite of the rigorous demands of Montanism, Christians flocked to the fledgling movement in Rome, Asia Minor, Africa, and Gaul, as persecution dogged the church from 177 CE on.

Left-behind theology was not the province of fringe groups alone, however. Names that still figure prominently in church history embraced a similar approach. Tertullian, one of the best known theologians in the history of the Western church, had a vision of a city descending over Judea every day for forty days and claimed, as a result, that the heavenly Jerusalem would soon descend. Justin Martyr argued that Christians would live for a thousand years in an earthbound, but transformed Jerusalem. Papias, believed to have been an acquaintance of John the Apostle, envisioned bunches of grapes vying for the attention of Jesus on the judgment day. And Irenaeus, famed Bishop of Lyons, borrowed freely on the same kind of images from both the Hebrew and the Greek Testaments. The trend continued throughout the Middle Ages and beyond. Drawing on both the Book of Revelation and other books both inside and outside of the biblical canon, the church continued to speculate about the shape of the future that lay ahead.

Inevitably, the interpretations varied with the circumstances faced by the visionaries. In France, apocalyptic speculations were tinged with dark expectations that reflected the bloodshed of the French Revolution. Convinced that no good could dominate without divine intervention, writers in the French church foresaw a future that could only be secured by the second coming of Christ. By contrast, in the fledgling American colonies that would become the United States, the expectations were initially optimistic. Buoyed by the conversions that took place in the Great Awakening, writers there anticipated a thousand-year reign ushered in by the colonists themselves.

Disappointments Great and Small

Nonetheless, left-behind theology remained a minority opinion in the life of the church and declined in popularity around the world. Even in the United States, where roadmap-readings had found a following in a culture marked by religious exploration, the speculative visions of apocalyptic writers floundered on the failed predictions of key religious leaders. The most notable of those failures was a prediction made by William Miller, a Baptist preacher from Vermont. Pressed for specifics by the members of his church, Miller had predicted that the second coming of Christ and the end of the world would come at last on October 22, 1844. The promised date passed and, dejected, Miller's followers abandoned their spiritual leader. This "Great Disappointment," as it was described, all but strangled the age-old roadmap approach to apocalyptic literature.

But then two changes breathed new life into the movement, one from within the movement, the other from without, and each was ideally suited to the other. First, the times changed. The optimism that had marked life in the United States gave way to the grim dislocation of civil war and the hope of heaven on earth evaporated. Alone, that change might have been fatal to the movement.

At the same time, however, left-behind theology changed as well and an approach called dispensationalism took the stage. In England, this new theology had been articulated by

Dispensationalism: the belief that biblical and human history consist of dispensations or eras that are divinely appointed

John Nelson Darby, who gave the new theology its name and basic character. Declaring biblical history and human history to consist, broadly speaking, of two dispensations or eras, Darby argued that the Bible described two attempts by God to redeem the human race, first through the Law and then through grace in Jesus Christ. On this basis, he further subdivided history into a series of smaller dispensations, including (at last) the events associated with the Book of Revelation and the end of all things.

More significantly, he set aside the historicist approach of his predecessors that had treated the events in Revelation as partially completed. This strategy had drawn the roadmap approach into question over and over again as each prediction of the end failed to materialize. By adopting a futurist perspective that treated the events described in Revelation as lying all but completely in the future, dispensationalism escaped the onus of failed predictions. Although a fine distinction, contemporary events appeared to weigh less immediately against the whole approach and created the impression that, if anything was amiss, it was probably the interpreter's reading of immediate future.

In the United States, this theology quickly took root with the aid of C. I. Scofield, who developed a study Bible that included notes describing Darby's approach alongside the text of Scripture. In this way dispensationalism was introduced *as Scripture was read*, rather than as a *means of understanding it or ordering its content*. Among its growing readership, the Scofield Study Bible gained the status of trusted guide and in some circles Scofield's notes were treated as if they enjoyed something of the same inspiration attributed to Scripture.

The new roadmap-reading of John's Apocalypse gained in popularity. Fueled by the vagaries of first the Civil War and then the dislocation of postwar reconstruction, Americans were drawn to the new approach as they reacted to the bruised and battered nation's ragged progress. The early decades of the twentieth century suggested further interpretive connections with the darker visions of the Apocalypse. The social dislocation brought on by growing urbanization and the Industrial Revolution produced economic dislocation, crime, and poverty that further erased any trace of the earlier hope that Americans would serve as God's servants in ushering in a new world order. Instead, the return of Christ became increasingly essential to any hope of change. Those convictions acquired specifically religious overtones with the early debates between modernists and fundamentalists over evolution, and the inspiration of Scripture began to draw attention. An ever-larger number of Bible readers concluded that they had good reason to believe that what was at stake was the eternal destiny of the world.

The two world wars served as a powerful catalyst for left-behind theologies. It was easy for those who followed roadmap-readings of Revelation to see in those events the potential for Armageddon.

But the two world wars that punctuated the first half of the new century served as a powerful catalyst for left-behind theologies. Because both wars involved much of the world, it was easy for those who followed roadmap-readings of Revelation to see in those events the potential for Armageddon. And Adolf Hitler's conduct offered the perfect model for that of an Antichrist. Both wars came and went, however, and with Hitler's death and defeat, the most plausible scenario for the end came and went as well.

A New Nation Breathes Life into an Old Movement

But events elsewhere in the world breathed new life into left-behind theology. Under what was called a "mandate," the British had governed Palestine and had sought for years to find a means of ameliorating the growing tensions between Jews and Arabs in the region. For two years following the end of World War II the British made a series of final attempts to draw the two groups together. Rebuffed first by one and then the other and haunted by some of their own history in the region, the British surrendered their mandate in November 1947. In response, the United Nations voted to partition the land west of the Jordan into two states, one Jewish and the other Arab, exercising by fiat the same kind of control that others had exercised in the region.

A new Israeli nation-state was born and with its rebirth, roadmap-readings of Revelation gained new impetus. This time, however, those readings were fueled by the conviction that the timetable of events its proponents anticipated would materialize in the Holy Land itself. Even the resulting conflict that erupted in the region generated further speculation. When the world's superpowers waded in, attempting to control the region's oil, it was clear to many, Armageddon was—at last—on its way.

Hard as it is to imagine, however, left-behind theology continued to be a minority movement well into the 1960s. Dispensationalists had gained a larger place in the Christian church thanks to the modernist-fundamentalist debate of the 1920s and the 1930s. With a common enemy in the modernist defense of evolution and critical approaches to Scripture, fundamentalists had struck an uneasy truce with dispensationalism in the name of battling what they perceived to be the more serious threat inherent in modern ideologies. Francis Patton, president of Princeton University and a conservative Presbyterian, was frequently an ally of dispensationalists but declared, "I am not foolish enough to be one of them." [4] J. Gresham Machen, theological defender of fundamentalist causes, observed:

> The recrudescence of "Chialism" or "premillenialism" in the modern church causes us serious concern; it is coupled we think, with a false method of interpreting Scripture which in the long run will be productive of harm. Yet how great is our agreement with those who hold the premillenial view . . . their error, serious though it may be, is not deadly error; and Christian fellowship with loyalty not only to the Bible but to the great creeds of the church, can still unite us with them. [5]

But this begrudging endorsement had not won dispensationalism a significantly larger following.

A Miracle of Marketing

But then a miracle of marketing intervened. Hal Lindsey, who had attended Dallas Theological Seminary (the modern academic home of dispensationalism), combined his class notes with an up-to-date roadmap-reading of the situation in Israel, the potential for nuclear Armageddon, and the arms race between the United States and the Soviet Union. Sold in a paperback edition alongside grocery store checkout counters, *The Late Great Planet Earth* sold millions of copies, was issued in thirteen different editions, and shaped a generation's thinking about the Book of Revelation. [6] The book's success left the impression that the dispensationalist approach to Revelation was the only way to read the book.

The Late Great Planet Earth sold millions of copies, was issued in thirteen different editions, and shaped a generation's thinking about the Book of Revelation.

In the years since, the political landscape has changed radically. Tensions in the Middle East continue unabated and will for the foreseeable future, but the shape of those tensions is radically different from the heyday of Lindsey's book. The Iron Curtain has disappeared, the Berlin Wall has been dismantled, and the Soviet Union is no more. It is no longer possible to imagine that the road ahead looks like the one that Lindsey described.

Nonetheless, his work so shaped the way in which people of every theological stripe read the Book of Revelation that today people are scarcely aware that there are alternatives. Those who do not read it in this way either do not read it at all or—like my students—they are afraid to read it, because they are convinced that it is the only alternative. So, as much as the political landscape has changed, writers continue to advance alternative roadmap-readings. Iran, Iraq, and Saddam Hussein are interchangeable pieces in a scenario that is reframed time and again, but never changes.

The Basics of Left-Behind Theology

For that reason the basic elements of left-behind salvation have remained remarkably stable across the centuries and across cultures, even though the details have changed:

> It is *"collective, in the sense that it is to be enjoyed by the faithful as a collectivity."* The righteous will be the beneficiaries of God's grace. In the judgment that is coming, they can rest assured of their fate. They can expect injustices to be corrected, and they can be confident that evil will be judged.
>
> It is *"terrestrial, in the sense that it is to be realized on this earth and not in some other-worldly heaven."* Heaven may follow, to be sure. But the vindication that the righteous expect will take place on this earth. Nations will fall, people will perish, the social and natural worlds around us will change.
>
> It is *"imminent, in the sense that it is to come both soon and suddenly."* There is no time to waste. Those who hope to participate in the victory of God should repent and respond to God's gracious offer now. The proximity of the end and our inability to predict its coming will spell the demise of many.
>
> It is *"total, in the sense that it is utterly to transform life on earth, so that the new dispensation will be no mere improvement on the present but perfection itself."* Piecemeal or temporary improvements are not enough. Repair will not do. If God is God, then the changes will be complete.
>
> And it is *"miraculous, in the sense that it is to be accomplished by, or with the help of, supernatural agencies."* The dimensions of the redress that are needed cannot be accomplished by human means. Only God can provide a way out.[7]

The communities that have grown up around these basic elements have varied. Some have observed an ascetic approach to life, choosing to set aside features of day-to-day existence that most of us take for granted: raising families, preparing for one kind of work or another, life in the mainstream of society. The Shakers, for example, whose communities were first established in the eighteenth century, observed a strict separation of the sexes and lived in self-sufficient communities, isolated from the rest of the world. The whole of their lifestyle was shaped by their roadmap, and they were convinced that the roadmap indicated that there was little history that lay ahead. Rearing children was unnecessary. The labor of the community was devoted to meeting the rather more immediate needs of the faithful. And even the architecture and furnishings of their lives reflected their convictions. The lives of most left-behind communities are, however, all but indistinguishable from the vast majority of people who live around them. Their members drive cars, pursue an education, raise their families, and buy homes. In spreading their message, they write and publish books, maintain websites and go to churches that look a great deal like the ones that we all attend. In spite of their differences, the Book of Revelation has been central to them all.

The communities that have grown up around these basic elements have varied. Some have observed an ascetic approach to life, choosing to set aside features of day-to-day existence that most of us take for granted.

STRENGTHS

As a result, roadmap communities have not found it difficult to incorporate this seemingly opaque biblical book into their theology. Nor have they found it difficult to explain how it speaks to their lives. Speaking as it does in immediate and urgent ways to their circumstances and to the condition of the world around them, they may puzzle about the meaning of this image or that, but these are people for whom the broader question of application is not in doubt. Illuminating the significance of world events, the Book of Revelation has been both a means of addressing any confusion that may exist about the world around them, providing both comfort and a stimulus for repentance.

Likewise, roadmap faith communities have had little or no difficulty in finding a place for the language of eschatology (the theology of last things). Judgment, salvation, heaven, and hell, as well as the final redress of injustices so often left unaddressed in our world, are all concerns that fit fairly seamlessly into the vocabulary of their faith. And given the prominence of such language in both testaments, as well as in the teaching of Jesus and Paul, roadmap-readings of Revelation make easy connections with other parts of the Bible.

STRUGGLES

If they have struggled, roadmap-readers have struggled to transcend the speculative nature of the interpretation their view has promoted. And apart from underlining the urgent need to repent, they have found it difficult to explain how Revelation speaks to the human condition.

As a result, the categories of judgment and of God-as-judge have dominated their theology. And whether they have intended it or not, the inevitable corollary has been a zero-sum spirituality in which roadmap-readings of Revelation appear to suggest: "I can't go to heaven, unless you go to hell." Communities built around that message also lack a clear reason to work for social justice. Knowing that "the end is near," there seems to be little or no need to work for change in a world that is about to evaporate, along with its injustices.

Eschatology: the branch of theology that concerns itself with the end of time

Of course, these struggles are all arguably questions of balance, rather than a matter of getting the book's meaning right. One might conceivably argue that the excesses of roadmap-readings are just that—excesses. The role of God as judge can be complemented by a vision of God's passion for redeeming humankind. The anticipated end of all things need not be thought of as an exemption from moral responsibility. The fact that Revelation does allow us to map our place in the divine agenda should not so overwhelm us that we become lost in fruitless speculation. It is this realization, of course, that has breathed life back into roadmap-readings over and over again. Specific interpretations may fall into disrepute. The approach does not. But balance is not the only issue.

Continuing the Conversation . . .

On the early history of roadmap-readings and left-behind theology, see McGinn, Bernard, *Apocalyptic Spirituality: Treatises of Lactantius, Adso of Montier-en-der, Joachim of Fiore, The Franciscan Spirituals, Savonarola* (The Classics of Western Spirituality; Mahwah, N.J.: Paulist Press, 1979); Eugene Weber, *Apocalypses: Prophesies, Cults, and Millennial Beliefs through the Ages.* (Cambridge: Harvard University Press, 1999).

Pivotal roadmap-readings include John N. Darby, *Lectures on the Second Coming* (repr.; London: G. Morrish, 1909); Cyrus I. Scofield, ed., *The Scofield Reference Bible: The Holy Bible containing the Old and New Testaments* (rev. ed.; New York: Oxford University Press, 1945); Hal Lindsey, *The Late Great Planet Earth* (New York: Bantam Books, 1973).

Roadmap-readings of John's Apocalypse have been particularly influential in the United States. On the history of their influence, see Paul Boyer, *When Time Shall Be No More: Prophecy Belief in Modern American Culture* (Cambridge, Mass.: Belknap Press, 1992); Amy Johnson Frykhom, *Rapture Culture: Left Behind in Evangelical America* (Oxford: Oxford University Press, 2004).

CHAPTER TWO

Revelation as Myth

When I was an adolescent I often competed in public speaking contests. Overly earnest and keen to be a diplomat when I grew up, I was convinced that experiences of that kind prepared me for the future. I can still remember the first speech: "Optimism, Youth's Greatest Asset," and I still remember how pleased I was to find a way to use the word *catalyst* in it!

When you are that interested in words that early in life, you tend to personalize your relationship with them. You might even tend to feel a bit sorry for some of them from time to time. After all, words are people, too! And the word *myth* has had a far more troubled life than it deserves. Often thought of today as synonymous with just one of its connotations, the idea that a myth is a falsehood has overrun its deeper and more noble meanings.

> The word myth *has had a far more troubled life than it deserves.*

Far from just a synonym for falsehood, myth is not just a fairy tale but is also a bit of narrative or an image used to describe in an evocative fashion the real and deeper nature of an experience, event, or person. We tell myths to conjure up a set of associations that not only pluck at our heartstrings, but also shape our thinking and prompt us to act. For that reason, perhaps it is not at all surprising to discover that some interpreters have argued that the true meaning of the Book of Revelation is not to be found in a one-to-one and literalistic decoding of the book's images, but in the evocative and symbolic character of its language.

We tell myths to conjure up a set of associations that not only pluck at our heartstrings, but also shape our thinking and prompt us to act.

I have chosen to call this a "mythic reading" of Revelation, because it speaks to the way in which these interpreters understand the language of the book. But there are other labels used to describe much the same thing, including poetic, idealist, spiritual, allegorical, and—most unwieldy of all—contemporary reinterpretation.

The Origen(s) of a Mythic Reading

Like roadmap-readings of John's Apocalypse, mythic readings have been around for a long time. In the third and fourth centuries, some of its leading advocates were bishops whose views were shaped by Origen, the great theologian and biblical scholar of the church who lived from 185 to 254 CE. All that remains of Origen's work on the Book of Revelation is part of a commentary. But it is not difficult to determine how he understood the book, because the fragments provide us with some clues and because Origen had a great deal to say about last things (or eschatology) as he found the subject elsewhere in Scripture.

Origen taught that Scripture possesses three kinds of meaning: the literal, the moral, and the spiritual or allegorical. Convinced that Scripture is inspired in a way that shapes not just the meaning of the text, but the choice and arrangement of words, Origen held that there is a message of benefit to the reader, no matter what appearances may suggest. The first and most obvious is to be found on the literal or surface level of the text. What we read there may be of immediate and obvious significance: shaping our beliefs, reminding us of the gospel's content and the work of Christ. If not, Origen noted, then the significance may be moral in character: speaking to the way in which we live, commending honesty, charity, and other virtues. Failing that, Scripture, according to Origen, still has some-

thing to teach us, but it is probably spiritual or allegorical in character. Hidden in the words and images used is still another message.

Origen also taught that this final level of meaning was, to some
degree, always present in the text. In fact, if a passage lacked any
dimension of value it was, according to Origen, probably the literal!
But the ability to find it rested in large part with the spiritual and
moral commitment of the reader and the guidance of the Holy
Spirit. For that reason, perhaps, Origen sometimes talked about
Scripture in even simpler terms, arguing that it has three dimensions: one a literal and theological; one literal and moral; and the
other a figurative and spiritual meaning.

Given his assumptions, it not surprising to find that Origen held
that most of the meaning to be culled from John's Apocalypse lay
primarily on a spiritual or allegorical level. After all, the language of
the book rarely lends itself to an obvious theological or moral reading and the obscurity of the images looks like part of a spiritual test!

Applied to John's Apocalypse, the images found there are, as a
result, treated like timeless ciphers, symbols that represent ideals and
types that can be applied with meaning to any day and age. So, for
example, when John writes that he saw a door to heaven open and
heard a voice like a silver trumpet, Origen is clear: there is no literal
door opened and the voice heard is not a literal trumpet. It is God's
Word, as the precious metal silver suggests (Rev 4:1; compare to Num
10:1ff.). And in Matthew 24 where similar language is used to describe
the Son of Man arriving on clouds "with power and great glory," Origen suggests that the clouds are, in all likelihood, a reference either to
"'holy and divine powers'" or the prophets of Israel.[1]

If Origen's approach sounds a bit Greek, that's because it is. Both
Jewish and Christian approaches to Scripture were profoundly
shaped by the high culture of Greece; and even though the nation of
Greece itself was long gone, its values interpenetrated the way in
which Christians read Scripture. This was particularly the case in
ancient Alexandria, Egypt, where Origen taught for years. The net
result was a religious and cultural amalgam that placed a premium
upon the spiritual over the material. Interpreters before and after
Origen often saw this world as filled with imperfect reflections of
eternal and perfect realities, much as the Greek philosopher Plato

believed that this world was an imperfect reflection of ideas in the mind of God.

Given his worldview, Origen was far more interested in the similarities between Scripture and the creative work of God, than he was in the character of the literature itself. When he talked about the three levels of Scripture's meaning, he often drew parallels with the tripartite nature of human kind, arguing that the literal, moral, and spiritual meanings of the Bible corresponded to the body, soul, and spirit that God gave to us. And when he talked about the two dimensions of Scripture, he often compared the literal and the spiritual to the human and the divine in the nature of Christ.

Thanks to the existing popularity of this approach and the powerfully persuasive character of Origen's work, mythic readings of Revelation held sway over large parts of the church for centuries. Dionysius, Bishop of Alexandria and Origen's disciple, lacked his mentor's intellectual gifts, but he shared his convictions about wherein the meaning lay. Commenting on John's Apocalypse, Dionysius observed, "I myself would never dare to reject the book [of Revelation], of which many good Christians have a very high opinion, but realizing that my mental powers are inadequate to judge it properly, I take the view that the interpretation of the various sections is largely a mystery, something too wonderful for our comprehension . . . but I suspect that some *deeper meaning* is concealed in the words."[2] And Eusebius, who was also a bishop of the church and an influential historian, inherited the same disaffection for roadmap-readings that Origen possessed, having been influenced by Dionysius.[3] Taking a second-century author to task, Eusebius writes:

> [Papias] says that after the resurrection of the dead there will be a period of a thousand years, when Christ's kingdom will be set up on this earth in material form. I suppose he got these notions by misinterpreting the apostolic accounts and failing to grasp what they said in mystic and symbolic language. For he seems to have been a man of very small intelligence, to judge from his books. But it is partly due to him that the great majority of churchmen after him took the same view.[4]

Eusebius himself says very little of a direct nature about the basis of his objections. At the time, Revelation's place as Scripture was in dispute and that may have shaped his views to some degree. But clearly he also found fault with the left-behind theology of his own day and that criticism seems to have been rooted in a misunderstanding of what he describes as the book's "mystic and symbolic language." His approach, however, and that of his mentors, Origen and Dionysius, was reinforced in significant ways by yet another bishop of the fifth century—the man who eventually would be known as Saint Augustine.

Augustine of Hippo

No ancient interpreter of Scripture shaped the approach to John's Apocalypse in quite the way that Augustine of Hippo did. By most scholars' estimates, the fact that it is in the Greek Testament at all is probably thanks to the efforts made by Augustine.

Well into the third century only occasional use had been made of John's Apocalypse and the surviving evidence seems to suggest that it was read more often in the western part of the church than in the eastern. When roadmap-readers began to object to the mythic approach nurtured by Origen, the latter's disciple, Dionysius, tried to head off a return to interpretations of that kind by raising questions about the book's authorship and its ties to the John of John's Gospel. Though by modern standards, he made some fairly telling arguments, he did not press his case too hard, because in the final analysis he was less interested in ending the church's use of the Apocalypse than he was in preventing a return to roadmap-readings of it.

As a result, Revelation was exposed to fresh controversy and it might have been pushed completely to the fringes of the church's life, had it not been for Augustine. Baptized in 387 CE and made coadjutor to Valerius, bishop of Hippo, in 395, Augustine exercised considerable influence over the life of the church from that point on. Making his views known in three provincial councils (or meetings) held to discuss the shape of the church's sacred literature, he insured that the twenty-seven books that make up today's Greek or New Testament canon are the ones we read today. The significance of the decision is not only clear in retrospect, but it was clear in prospect as well. The accompanying legislation passed by the last two councils held in Carthage in 393 and 397 declared, "Besides the canonical

Scriptures, nothing shall be read in church under the name of the divine Scriptures."[5]

In all likelihood, Augustine had a number of reasons for supporting the inclusion of Revelation in the fledgling church's Scriptures. One was probably practical. The debate over the status of the literature used by the church in worship had been a long one and a certain amount of clarity about what would and would not be used in that fashion was probably desirable from Augustine's point of view. As biblical scholar Bruce Metzger observes, "The debate of so many generations was practically over. But it remained for some one to say that it was over."[6] Augustine did just that. And—although he was undoubtedly mistaken—the Bishop of Hippo shared the conviction of some that the author of the Apocalypse was the author of the Fourth Gospel and that both were the Apostle John. So he didn't have the same doubts about the book that some of his contemporaries entertained.

The Apocalypse also fit well with the theological views of Augustine, so he had no particular qualms about the content of the book. In fact, one could say that it actually spoke so directly to parts of his theological outlook that he must have strongly favored its being used. In his work *The City of God*, Augustine tells the story of God's effort to redeem humankind working in and through history. For the Bishop of Hippo, sacred literature was not something read as a product of history or as literature of varying kinds, it was the story of that redemptive effort and should be read as such. Scripture spoke to the lives of those who read it, but it also told the parts of the story, both past and future, that its readers did not and could not know. For Augustine, that sacred history consisted of six parts: from Adam to Noah, Noah to Abraham, Abraham to David, David to the captivity in Babylon, the captivity to the birth of Christ, and the birth of Christ to the Last Judgment. The Apocalypse clearly contributed to telling the entire story.

> In all likelihood, Augustine had a number of reasons for supporting the inclusion of Revelation in the fledgling church's Scriptures.

But Augustine did not read Revelation in literalistic terms. In his history of God's redemptive efforts, the city of God and that of the world stood in sharp contrast. He even compared the latter to the beast from the sea in Rev 13:1. But he didn't think for a moment that there was one city and one beast, nor did he believe that the city was a beast in any literal sense at all. Instead, for Augustine, any number of empires that didn't know God and refused to repent deserved that description, including Assyria, Athens, and Rome. And the bishop believed that this list would expand endlessly until the end of all things. In the meantime, there would be Armageddon, or war, but that war was the struggle for righteousness fought out between those who occupied the two cities: "It is therefore of this kingdom at war, in which conflict still rages with the enemy, that the Apocalypse is speaking in the passage we are considering. In this kingdom sometimes there is fighting against vices that attack us, though sometimes they submit to being ruled, until that kingdom of perfect peace comes where the King will reign without opposition."[7]

> And I saw a beast rising out of the sea, having ten horns and seven heads; and on its horns were ten diadems, and on its heads were blasphemous names. —REV 13:1

Augustine's approach would dominate the church's interpretation of John's Apocalypse until the late twelfth century, shaping some of the earliest Latin commentaries on Scripture ever written on the book. And during that time the mythic approach to Scripture was generally shaped by the same convictions that led Augustine to champion the Apocalypse's place in the canon:

- Scripture tells the story of God's redemptive effort.
- It should be read as such.
- The images found in Revelation speak in mythic terms describing God's final triumph, or they describe the struggle in the time being.

Myth and the Modern Interpreter

Since that time the mythic approach has been used less often than it was during the first twelve centuries of the church's life. In part, the movement away from such readings can be traced to changes in the church's view of Scripture, which we will discuss at greater length in the next chapter. Suffice it to say here that an ever-greater number of scholars concluded that the biblical text could not be read simply and flatly as a straightforward record of God's redemptive efforts, nor could it be read without attention to historical context. Those conclusions alone made it difficult to think of any book—John's Apocalypse included—as a montage of timeless ciphers. Biblical scholars would eventually reconsider the importance of myth, but most would never again embrace Augustine's assumptions about Scripture.

In addition, the emergence of a new approach to roadmap-readings in the twelfth century also helped to polarize the debate over the nature of John's message. Roadmap-readings of Revelation had never disappeared, and in the coming of the year 1000 CE, apocalyptic enthusiasm and predictions of the world's end flourished. The passing of Haley's comet fueled speculation in 989. When the feast of the Annunciation and Good Friday occurred on the same day in 992, there were those who predicted that the world would end within three years. And when the year 1000 came and went without incident, some shifted their attention to the millennial anniversary of Christ's passion in 1033.

Feast of the Annunciation: the annual celebration of Mary's acceptance of the angel's announcement that she was to bear the child Jesus.

These, however, were all predictions of an end that would come in a single moment. In the twelfth century, Joachim of Fiore, a Franciscan monk, changed all of that, reading Scripture instead as a window into history. Dividing the human experience into three eras, each corresponding to a member of the Trinity, Joachim argued that the history of humankind could be traced in Scripture and that the church could anticipate a series of events in advance of the end. This approach broke with the tradition begun by Augustine, whose work had an "individualizing and moralizing" impact on the church's reading of Revelation, and gave permission in new ways for roadmap-readings of the text.

As a result, roadmap-readings and what I describe in the next chapter as "historical readings" became the dominant alternatives. By contrast, mythic readings lost ground to the debate. On one hand, those who favored a roadmap approach tended to equate myth with falsehood. If what John described wasn't real, then it wasn't true and that conclusion was hardly acceptable. On the other hand, historians who felt the meaning of the text was to be found in its historical setting felt that the mythic approach popularized by Augustine was naïve in its use of Scripture. John may have used myth, but he was hardly focused on eternal verities.

(More or Less) Modern Mythic Readings

This is not to say that mythic readings have completely disappeared. But they no longer share the common convictions that shaped the earlier interpretations offered by Origen, Dionysius, Eusebius, Augustine, and others. Instead, the readings are scattered and the working assumptions behind them vary greatly.

One example is the reading provided by Jacques Ellul in his book *Apocalypse: The Book of Revelation*, first published in French in 1975 and then in English in 1977.[8] Ellul was well known as a professor of law, a sociologist, a historian, politician, and lay theologian. His circle of influence included lawyer-turned-theologian William Stringfellow and one-time president of the United States Jimmy Carter.

His work was deeply shaped by exposure to Karl Marx, whose critique of economic structures impressed him, and by the Swiss theologian Karl Barth, whose work he emulated. His perspective on the world was also profoundly influenced by his involvement in the French resistance during World War II, through which he helped Jewish refugees escape the German SS. When the war ended with the dropping of atomic bombs at Nagasaki and Hiroshima, Ellul declared that, contrary to all appearances, Nazi Germany had won, declaring:

> In this terrible dance of means which have been unleashed, no one knows where we are going, the end has been left behind. Humanity has set out at tremendous speed—to go nowhere. . . . Everything that "succeeds," everything that is effective, everything in itself "efficient," is justified.[9]

Predisposed to think in dialectical terms—meaning that he cast things in either/or categories—much of his theological work was considered contentious and lacking in nuance. He also angered biblical scholars and often suggested that the absence of a relationship with God insured that they could not understand Scripture properly, in spite of all their learning. As a result he drew no small amount of attention when, at age sixty-five, his first book ever on the Bible was a commentary on John's Apocalypse.

What is less surprising, perhaps, is to discover that his reading of Revelation was anything but conventional. Ellul is aware of how the Book of Revelation has been read. He consciously rejects the notion of "deciphering" symbols in the way that a roadmap-reading would decode images. And, although he has clearly drawn upon historical approaches to the literature, nonetheless, he notes that there is already an ample number of what he describes as "scientific" commentaries on the text.

More to the point, however, Ellul believes that the purpose of Revelation—and not just the name of the book—is revelation. So, a historical reading of John's Apocalypse undermines the book's ability to speak to us. John wrote to change our behavior and if we only look to the past, then the book's purpose is lost.

Ellul believes that the purpose of Revelation—and not just the name of the book—is revelation. So, a historical reading of John's Apocalypse undermines the book's ability to speak to us.

So, what Ellul proposes to do is to move "dialectically" (i.e., to go back and forth) between the concrete political realities of his own day and the Book of Revelation, attempting to see the one in light of the other. For that reason, when Ellul begins to describe specific features of the book, he moves freely between observations that sound as if they are about the past, the present, and the timeless—all at the same time. And the evocative character of the images looms larger than any specifics that might be offered.

Commenting, for example, on the beasts mentioned in Rev 13, Ellul observes that the image with ten horns and seven heads *might* refer to Rome, but it is not limited to it. In the final analysis the horn is "the symbol of Power" and "multiplied by ten." It is "power carried to the absolute." Rome is, according to Ellul, simply the first of many such powers to which the Book of Revelation refers.[10] Similarly, the

He seized the dragon, that ancient serpent, who is the Devil and Satan, and bound him for a thousand years . . .
—REV 20:2

thousand-year reign described in chapter 20 may have its roots in historical experiences, but it is, more importantly, an image used to describe human effort whenever it is free of Satan's control. In such cases, "*love* and *reconciliation*" characterize human behavior and are expressed in "fraternity, solidarity, with the poor and weak, the movement toward a pure and idealistic socialism, and nonviolence."[11]

By setting the historical aside in this way, Ellul admits that what he is offering is a "naïve reading" of John's Apocalypse. But it is not, he argues, a completely naïve one. It is the naïveté of "one who, having known the interpretations fairly well, takes up everything again with an eye he wishes were new."[12]

When he does bring a new eye to the book as a whole, what Ellul sees is a complex structure of five sections, each containing seven elements of a different kind: messages, seals, trumpets, bowls, and visions. The first and the fifth sections are, respectively, descriptions of the church as it is now and the church as it shall be. The second and the fourth deal with the meaning of history and its end. The third and central section is the "axis" of John's vision and, according to Ellul, describes Jesus as Lord of both the church and of history. The very structure of the book is, in other words, an allegory of who the Lord is and of what he does. Reigning over history and the church in absolute freedom, the glorified Christ is a source of hope to those who acknowledge his lordship and is a judge to those who deny it.

More recently, Catherine Keller has taken a completely different approach to the mythic character of John's Apocalypse. Keller, like Ellul, is aware of the roadmap and historical approaches to the book, but her views of how Scripture should be read are decisively influenced by a feminist and post-structuralist (the view that meaning is not to be found in the words of a writer, but in the reader's inner dialogue with the words) point of view. This means that two lenses shape her reading of the book.

Post-structuralist: the belief that meaning isn't to be found in the words of a writer, but in the reader's own inner dialogue with those words

As a feminist, she is keenly aware of the way in which social context and, in particular, differences in gender have shaped the writing of biblical books. The Bible no less than any other literature has been shaped by the perspectives and goals of its writers, and those perspectives and goals are always "engendered"; that is, they are shaped by what it means to be either a man or a woman.

As a post-structuralist, she believes that the meaning we derive from reading Scripture arises not so much out of what appears on the page, but the conversation that each reader has with Scripture. Like Ellul, she knows the historical literature on John's Apocalypse, but she sets it aside for very different reasons. For Keller the issue is not that one needs to know God in order to understand Scripture. The effort to recover the historical meaning of Scripture is itself misguided. Meaning arises not so much out of what a piece of literature might have said to another generation, as it does out of our reading and interaction with the text. It is, in other words, a bit like reporting on what you make of an inkblot in a Rorschach test. There is no right or wrong way to read the book. The way you read it is just that—the way you read it.

Together, these commitments make Keller's effort a challenging book to read and all but impossible to outline in any traditional sense of the word. She rightly describes the result as kaleidoscopic and it is, leaving the reader with a series of discreet impressions that are as difficult to assimilate as the images used by John.[13] But the mythic looms large. So, for example, in describing the whore of Babylon, who appears in Rev 17, Keller argues that the similarity between the whore and Aphrodite evokes the image of goddess-murder and underlines John's inability to transcend his own engendered male perspective.

> *Keller believes that the meaning we derive from reading Scripture arises not so much out of what appears on the page, but the conversation that each reader has with Scripture.*

Similarly, in the arrival of a new earth described in Rev 21, Keller observes, "Like an old, used up wife, the consumed matrix of life is cast aside."[14]

These and other observations prompt her to assume a cautious relationship with John's Apocalypse and this may indeed be the central point of her work: one can neither surrender freely to the expectations and values of John's Apocalypse, nor abandon them entirely. "Our history cannot delete it without committing it" and so it must be "preserved and transcended."[15]

STRENGTHS

Given the considerable diversity of mythic readings, it is difficult to talk about the strengths and struggles of this approach in any kind of collective fashion. It is safe to say that the approach in all its forms responds to a dimension of John's Apocalypse that is central to its character. Make of it what you will, the evocative character of the images there demands an approach that is not tied to a literalistic approach.

In addition, most if not all of the mythic approaches also appreciate that the language used in the Book of Revelation works on more than one level. Even in those cases in which the images refer to a historical event, the imagery used also refers to something more allusive and suggestive of realities that cannot be exhausted by identifying a specific referent.

One can neither surrender freely to the expectations and values of John's Apocalypse, nor abandon them entirely.

As a result, the mythic approach can also be readily applied to questions of contemporary relevance, so in some ways both God and God's guidance are available in the same ready fashion that God and God's guidance are available in the roadmap approach. The difference is that the spiritual center of that guidance lies not in a particular interpretation of the events transpiring around the reader, but in the timeless assessment that God provides of certain patterns and tendencies. The roadmap-reader looks for an event that reflects the predictions found in Revelation, the mythic reader looks for the patterns that reappear time and time again throughout history that are either reflective of God's presence or in opposition to it.

STRUGGLES

As readily applicable as the mythic approach is, it achieves that application by ignoring the particular character of the book's original message. In the cases of Origen, Augustine, and even Ellul, this is a function of their conviction that God speaks through Scripture to some degree without reference to its historical setting. For Keller it is a function of broader social and philosophical assumptions arising out of her commitments to feminism and post-structuralism. As a result, all four make selective use of the history, but they are never consistent in their approach.

Beyond that shared struggle, however, mythic interpreters then differ in the way those struggles take shape, owing in large part to the very different set of assumptions that guide their work. Early mythic interpreters (Origen and Augustine among them) overlook the complexity of the biblical text. The doctrinal convictions that they bring to Scripture tend to treat the whole of the Bible as if it were untouched by human hands and communities. So, as a result, the peculiarities that are rooted in the character of the authors and the shape of their historical settings are largely suppressed or missed.

Later interpreters, including Ellul and Keller, are very clear about the complexities, but (for very different reasons) they are skeptical that those complexities offer much in the process of interpretation: Ellul because read in that way, one does not hear the voice of God in Scripture; Keller because the meaning is not to be found in trying to discern what the writer might have meant, but in the reading that we do now. As a result, for both Ellul and Keller the difficulty can be that in reading Scripture this way, there are any number of agendas that can be consciously or unconsciously substituted for what the writer intended. Just how that difficulty can be addressed is discussed in the next chapter.

Continuing the Conversation . . .

For other mythic readings, see Sam Hamstra Jr., "An Idealist View of Revelation," in *Four Views on the Book of Revelation* (ed. C. Marvin Pate; Grand Rapids: Zondervan, 1998); Paul S. Minear, *I Saw a New Earth: An Introduction to the Visions of the Apocalypse* (Washington: Corpus Books, 1968).

On Origen's approach to Scripture, see R. P. C. Hanson, *Allegory and Event: A Study of the Sources and Significance of Origen's Interpretation of Scripture* (Louisville: Westminster John Knox Press, 2002); Manlio Simonetti, *Biblical Interpretation in the Early Church: An Historical Introduction to Patristic Exegesis* (trans. Johan A. Hughes; ed. Anders Bergquist and Markus Bockmuehl; Edinburgh: T&T Clark, 1994).

CHAPTER THREE

Revelation as History

Anyone who has ever written a book knows how important an editor is. After writing for a while you learn that one of the problems you face as an author is that you see what you expect to see and not what appears on the printed page. So, even with reading after reading, a writer can fail to identify typographical errors and broken sentence construction. Editors see the manuscript with fresh eyes, and they often catch problems that have been there for months.

History Then and Now

Similarly, the early stories we are told about the history of biblical interpretation can shape what we see, even if there is very little evidence to justify that impression. That is particularly the case as it applies to the enterprise of historical criticism (the approach to Scripture that relies upon the historical setting of a text as an important key to its meaning). It is now so common to meet people who are convinced that historical approaches to the biblical text have their roots in the Enlightenment that it really no longer matters where the impression originated. And everyone has suffered for it.

Having been taught that this is the case, some people assume that an open, trusting approach to Scripture began with the disciples, if not Jesus himself, and continued to shape the life of the church in at least some circles until the seventeenth century. At that point, so the story goes, agnostic scholars conspired to expose Scripture to the light of historical examination in the hopes of undermining the church's influence. Nothing could be further from the truth.

To be sure, there are significant and useful insights that shaped historical inquiry in new ways that arose out of the Enlightenment and that justify the use of the phrase "historical-critical" to describe them. Ancient conceptions of history are also very different from the ones used today. And it is probably also fair to say that although the ancient world took history no less seriously than we do, ancient writers did not treat the text as part of the evidence in an effort to reconstruct what happened. And during the Enlightenment there were agnostics and atheists who studied Scripture, some of whom were, no doubt, hostile to the Christian faith. It could also be said that ancient interpreters were, generally speaking, more interested in the significance of what happened than they were in what actually happened.

> *As early as the second century, Christians raised questions about the authorship of Revelation.*

But, in fact, an interest in the historical issues surrounding John's Apocalypse is as old as either one of the approaches we have already examined and that interest has been just as much a concern for those living within the church as it has been for those outside. As early as the second century, Christians raised questions about the authorship of Revelation. A presbyter named Gaius expressed doubts about the book's apostolic connections. Eusebius, the church historian, offered observations about the circumstances under which the book was written. And, according to Eusebius, Dionysius, the bishop of Alexandria whom we have already mentioned, expressed concerns about both its theological content and its authorship:

> Farther on he has this to say about the Revelation of John: Some of our predecessors rejected the book and pulled it entirely to pieces, criticizing it chapter by chapter, pronouncing it unintelligible and illogical and the title false. They say it is not John's and is not a revelation at all, since it is heavily veiled by its thick curtain of incomprehensibility: so

far from being one of the apostles, the author of the book was not even one of the saints, or a member of the Church, but Cerinthus, the founder of the sect called Cerinthian after him, who wished to attach a name commanding respect to his own creation. This, they say, was the doctrine that he taught—that Christ's kingdom would be on earth; and the things he lusted after himself, being the slave of his body and sensual through and through, filled the heaven of his dreams—unlimited indulgence in gluttony and lechery at banquets, drinking-bouts, and wedding feasts, or (to call these things by what he thought more respectable names) festivals, sacrifices, and the immolation of victims.[1]

So, in describing a historical-critical approach to John's Apocalypse, I want to be careful not to suggest that it is an utterly new or modern phenomenon. That said, the contemporary enterprise does have a very different shape and it is important to know what the words *historical* and *critical* mean.

HISTORICAL

The adjective *historical* refers to the method's interest in discovering the intended meaning of the text. It focuses on the original writer and readers, as well as the historical, social, cultural, and religious circumstances that gave rise to the text being studied. Revered as they are today, it is very easy to forget that biblical texts were once very much like the writing we do today. Certain circumstances usually require us to write and we write in hopes of shaping the circumstances.

Historical critics give attention to that reality as a key to recovering the meaning of the Bible's literature. Far from being abstract, theological treatises, the books of the Bible are occasional pieces of literature, written to specific people, dealing with specific struggles, events, and controversies. Knowing as much as possible about those matters informs the interpreter's study of a given text. So, more often than not, they begin with five basic questions: who, what, where, when, and why? Unfortunately, the biblical writer is rarely explicit about those issues, and even when one is, there are almost always other agendas at work, some of which the writer may not even be able to name. Given the obscure,

Revered as they are today, it is very easy to forget that biblical texts were once very much like the writing we do today.

almost opaque character of the imagery used, this is particularly true of John's Apocalypse. Scholars are forced to work backward from the clues that the text gives them (i.e., *internal* evidence) and compare it with information that we have about the period from other sources (i.e., *external* evidence). In this case, the clues from the Bible that loom large are these:

- The name John (Rev 1:1, 4, 9)
- The reference to the Island of Patmos (Rev 1:9)
- The seven letters to the seven churches (Rev 2:1–3:22)
- References to Rome (Rev 13, 17, 18)
- References to eight Roman emperors or kings (Rev 17:8)
- A description of the eighth as one of the seven who returns (Rev 17:11)
- The identification of Rome with Babylon (Rev 17:5, 9, 18)

Not all of that evidence is useful in locating the book historically. To some early readers the reference to John immediately suggested connections with the apostle John, whose name is also associated with the fourth gospel and with three letters in the Greek Testament (1, 2, and 3 John). But the Apocalypse itself does not make that claim; ancient church leaders differed on the subject and some traditions suggest that John died in 70 CE. In addition, the Book of Revelation is of such a completely different style, vocabulary, and theological bent from John's Gospel that if the Gospel was influenced at all by the apostle, then it is all but certain that the same person did not write the Apocalypse. So all that scholars can know about *who* wrote the book was that his name was John and he considered himself a prophet.

All that scholars can know about who wrote the book of Revelation was that his name was John and he considered himself a prophet.

The references to Patmos and the seven churches help to some degree in locating the work geographically and thus answering the question, "Where?" The island of Patmos is thirty-seven miles southwest of Miletus, which is located on the western coast of Asia Minor (today, Turkey), and the seven churches mentioned are located in Asia Minor as well. During the first century, Asia Minor was at the heart of not only the Christian church but of Roman life as well. The world in which John lived was a point of natural intersection between the two, and any references that bear on the climate of that relationship would be entirely understandable.

The references that John makes to Rome and Roman emperors are of even greater help, because they situate the book against the backdrop of known history and provide some possible answers to the question of *when* the book was written. Rome's Empire period stretched from the rule of Julius Caesar who died in 44 BCE to the end of Trajan's rule in 117 CE and the dynasties as well as the reign of three "short-lived" emperors can be outlined with reasonable confidence:

44 BCE	Julius Caesar (died)
27 BCE–14 CE	Augustus
14–37 CE	Tiberius
37–41 CE	Gaius (Caligula)
41–54 CE	Claudius
54–68 CE	Nero
68–69 CE	Galba
69 CE	Otho
69 CE	Vitellius
69–79 CE	Vespasian
79–81 CE	Titus
81–96 CE	Domitian
96–98 CE	Nerva
98–117 CE	Trajan

John says that five of the seven kings or emperors "have fallen, one is living, and the other has not yet come; and when he comes, he must remain only a little while. As for the beast that was and is not, it is an eighth but it belongs to the seven, and it goes to destruction" (Rev 17:10–11). By referring to an eighth emperor who is simply one of the seven who returns, John helps to further narrow the range of possibilities, because—as most scholars agree—this is undoubtedly a reference to Nero. Infamous for what eventually became a chaotic and despotic era in Roman history, his fate in the wake of a death sentence from the Roman Senate was unknown. And, so legend had it that Nero would return. John's reference to the eighth ruler as "Nero-all-over-again," suggests that his reign is in the past and the legend was fairly current, so one has to imagine a date later than 68 CE.

As for the beast that was and is not, it is an eighth but it belongs to the seven, and it goes to destruction.

—REV 17:11

For some scholars, the time frame is further narrowed by the reference to Rome as the whore of Babylon (Rev 17:5). This seems to be a reference to Rome after the destruction of the Temple in Jerusalem, which would have prompted the comparison with Babylon's conquest of the city in 586 BCE. Since the Romans attacked Jerusalem in 70 CE, a number of scholars look for a date and setting in the last three decades of the century.

The only other clue that we have comes again from Rev 17:10, in which John says that five of the kings have fallen and one is living. So, presumably John is writing in the reign of the sixth emperor. There are, however, two problems: John does not tell us where to start counting and he doesn't tell us which emperors are on his list! So, it is here that historians focus on trying to solve the problem of dating and it is here that they differ most, each relying more heavily on some pieces of evidence than others.

A variety of theories have been advanced, but two schools of thought have prevailed among scholars. From the second century through the nineteenth and now, again, in the twentieth and twenty-first, the majority of scholars have favored a dating to the reign of the Emperor Domitian (81–96 CE). These scholars assume that John didn't count all of the emperors and probably selected them for a variety of reasons. For example, he may have excluded the reigns of Galba, Otho, and Vitellius from his list because their time in office was so brief; and, more importantly, he may have included others because their insistence on emperor worship would have entitled them to the epithet "Antichrist." For some of these scholars, the second-century testimony of Iranaeus, who said that John wrote during the reign of Domitian, is decisive in helping to interpret the internal evidence.

During the nineteenth century, however, a number of scholars believed—and some still do—that the social dislocation at the end of Nero's reign and the beginning of Galba's brief tenure in office are a better fit with the turmoil to which the Apocalypse refers. So, beginning either with Julius Caesar or Caesar Augustus, they count forward, including all of the names. Of course, in so doing, they choose

to discount the external evidence from Iranaeus (which also identifies John the Apostle as the author). They minimize the allusion to
"Nero-all-over-again"—or assume that the legend spread much more
quickly. And, while they still believe that John thought of Rome and
the whore of Babylon, they minimize the significance of Jerusalem's
destruction in 70 CE as the impetus for that comparison.

All in all, then, a somewhat stronger argument is to be made for
those who date the Apocalypse to the reign of Domitian. But the question of *what* prompted John to write presents yet another puzzle.

Interpreters once assumed that Domitian's reign was marked by
egregious brutality and, for that reason, attributed the crisis alluded
to in Revelation to widespread persecution of the church. So when
an older generation of scholars suggested that John wrote in the
wake of Roman persecution, most of us conjure up visions of colos-
seums choked with bloodthirsty spectators and hapless Christians
facing lions.

This impression was largely shaped by the historian Eusebius who
referred to the "appalling cruelty of Domitian" and argued that
John's exile to Patmos was representative of that cruelty. But closer
scrutiny of Eusebius's account has raised serious questions about its
veracity. The great church historian wrote long after the time of
Domitian, so he lacked any first-hand knowledge of the emperor's
behavior. More importantly, Eusebius relied heavily on Roman
sources that were colored by the political agendas of their authors,
who worked very hard to ingratiate themselves with Domitian's suc-
cessors. They had every reason to cast the emperor in a negative light
and, given the contradictions in their reports, they probably did.

As a result, historians have concluded that the occasion for the
book was something rather subtler, which certainly provoked concern, but may not have amounted to large-scale persecutions of the
kind that scholars once imagined were contemporary with John's
day. This is not to say that the church had not experienced persecution of that kind. In fact, the memory of it was probably fairly vivid.
But the sense of tension, crisis, and alienation that John and some of
his circle felt is traceable to other factors as well.

One was a regional enthusiasm for emperor worship and the
implied pressure to participate. There is no decisive evidence to sug-

gest that Domitian demanded more attention to the emperor cult than did his predecessors. But literature from the period suggests that emperor worship remained an expression of patriotism and a means by which provinces sought to ingratiate themselves to the emperor. One need not imagine that Roman citizens gang-pressed Christians into such worship to conclude that there was considerable social pressure to conform. No one who has ever watched public displays of religious or national loyalty needs to be told how much informal pressure can be brought to bear on those who refuse to participate.

Closely allied to this dynamic were localized, informal persecutions that Christians experienced as part and parcel of the hostile reaction to the exclusivity of their religious practice. The literature of the period suggests that Roman suspicions about their Christian neighbors were marked by just the kind of stereotypes, prejudices, and rumors that usually accompany such treatment. So it is not necessary to imagine that Christians were subjected to formal persecution. It is much more likely, in fact, that they were regularly subjected to regional and informal mistreatment.

A third factor was the changing shape of the Christian community's relationship with Judaism. For much of the first century, early Christians were considered a Jewish sect and that identity deeply shaped the consciousness of the first Christians. They lived as Jews, worshiped with Jews, and enjoyed the exemption from practices like emperor worship. But near the end of the century when John wrote his Apocalypse, Christians were expelled from Jewish synagogues across the Mediterranean world. This not only thrust the church into new tensions with the Roman world around them, but it also introduced new tensions with the Jewish community. The church was wounded by the expulsion, and struggled to define itself in the wake of those changes.

For much of the first century, early Christians were considered a Jewish sect and that identity deeply shaped the consciousness of the first Christians.

To say that none of this required John to see the situation in such dire terms is to underline the fact that biblical literature is not just a product of the historical circumstances to which it was addressed, but represents as well the writer's attempt to shape the perceptions of those around him. Indeed, yet another important dimension of the crisis from

John's point of view was the fact that not all Christians reacted to it in the same way or, for that matter, saw the situation as a crisis. This is clear, in particular, from the letters to the church in Laodicea (Rev 3:14–22).

On every side, then, the result was a clash of "symbolic worlds" that, for John, represented in some senses a far more acute challenge to the life of the church than an organized persecution would have caused. From his point of view, the struggle was all the more difficult because the crisis presented itself in such a subtle fashion and because it drew his community into conflict—not just with Rome or with the Judaism with which it so strongly identified—but with the Christian community itself. As such the Apocalypse is both a call for faithfulness under circumstances that he feared would erode the commitment of the community and an effort to shape the perceptions of that community in a fashion that would prompt it to take that call seriously.

> "I know your works; you are neither cold nor hot. I wish that you were either cold or hot. So, because you are lukewarm, and neither cold nor hot, I am about to spit you out of my mouth."
> —REV 3:15–16

CRITICAL

Locating the biblical text in such a concrete fashion in the day-to-day affairs of real people, times, places, and concerns can suggest to some that the word *critical* in the phrase *historical-critical* is largely negative in character. It is not uncommon to find people who believe that the enterprise I have described is part and parcel of the Enlightenment conspiracy that I described at the beginning of the chapter: an effort designed to rob Scripture of its authority by "bringing it down on our level" and treating it as human words about a human situation.

> **Apocalypse:** a word with three meanings. (1) It may refer to the end of the world, and the salvation of the righteous, or (2) it may be used to describe a type of literature emphasizing the "unveiling" of divine mysteries, and (3) it refers to a specific book written in that form, such as the Book of Revelation.

But the word *critical* is not used to mean "captious" or "fault-finding." The historical critic is one who goes about her or his task in a "thinking" or "discerning" fashion. As such, the contribution that the scholar seeks to make is inherently positive. And the goal in view is to weigh the evidence that historical study makes available in order to arrive at new certainties, or as much certainty as is possible, knowing that all historical study is based upon probabilities. It might be true that some biblical critics have been skeptics at times, but there is no necessary connection between the practice of criticism and a loss of faith, let alone hostility to it.

Nor is the historical-critical approach more or less susceptible to misuse than is any other approach to the task, including an approach governed by no method at all. Indeed, because historical data is the common property of anyone prepared to take the time and effort necessary to master it, the critical approach is, in fact, an advance over other methods. For when interpretations are offered without attention to the writer's intended meaning, one understanding is as good as the next, the historical-critical method requires both parties to defend their views on the basis of method and evidence.

> *It might be true that some biblical critics have been skeptics at times, but there is no necessary connection between the practice of criticism and a loss of faith, let alone hostility to it.*

This is why a critical reading of the Bible (in the best sense of the word) goes beyond a careful reading of the text alone. Ultimately, the critical process of raising and answering questions should involve probing not only the words and worlds of the biblical text, but the information and perspectives that will help us to understand those worlds more completely. Applied to John's Apocalypse, this means that the historical critic sees and treats this literature as the product of a particular time and place, addressed in the first place to that time and place. The tools used to understand that literature are as varied as the tools used with any piece of literature.

So critics use textual criticism (the study of ancient manuscripts to insure that we know as closely as possible what the original said in Greek, Hebrew, or Aramaic) to see to it that the text we use is as accurate as possible. They rely on literary criticism (the study of language, genre, and style as a key to discovering an author's meaning) to ask questions about the nature (or genre) and structure of the literature, including the use of myth that (as we have observed) other approaches emphasize. And they use sociological criticism (a study of texts of the Bible as a window into the social order and interaction that shaped the communities in which the texts were written) to unpack the dynamics at work in the communities reflected in the literature.

These and other tools are used because scholars believe that God speaks to us *in and through life*. For Anglicans, in particular, this is a part of our theological heritage. The incarnation is not simply a doctrine that describes the nature of Christ's work in the world, but captures, as well, the way in which God is always at work in the world. And it is this realization that should guide us in deciding how to read John's Apocalypse.

Leaving Behind Left Behind

Years ago I regularly taught a course for undergraduates dealing in part with the Book of Revelation. I soon discovered that there was almost no means of teaching that class without doing exactly what we have just done in the first three chapters of this brief book. I took time to talk in detail about roadmap, mythic, and historical readings and then, as now, I turned to the question of how we ourselves might evaluate the approaches available to us.

Much to my students' surprise, I almost always started the class with a brief film clip from Metro-Goldwyn-Mayer's production of *The Wizard of Oz*, starring Judy Garland, Jack Haley, Bert Lahr, and Ray Bolger. More often than not I used early scenes of the movie, including the ones with the tornado bearing down on Dorothy's home in rural Kansas; Bert Lahr crying out, "It's a twister, It's a twister!"; Dorothy's failed attempt to enter the storm cellar; her effort to take shelter in the house; the flying window frame that hits Dorothy in the head; Dorothy's dreamed-of flight to Oz on the tornado's wind; and her crash landing in Munchkinland. I almost always waited for the Munchkins to sing, "Ding Dong! The witch is dead." before I brought the movie to a stop.

> The incarnation is not simply a doctrine that describes the nature of Christ's work in the world, but captures, as well, the way in which God is always at work in the world.

Then, I would ask the students to tell me what they thought the movie was all about. There was always a variety of answers, but responses inevitably included Dorothy's immortal line, "There's no place like home." Others usually noted that the gifts everyone sought were gifts they already possessed within: the Tin Man really had a heart; the Scarecrow really had a brain; and the Lion really did possess courage.

When we had exhausted the possible meanings, I would usually ask them if they had ever read the book behind the movie.[2] The

41

answer was usually, "No." And then I would introduce them to the scholarship on the book, which at the time suggested that L. Frank Baum, the story's author, didn't write a children's story at all, or did so secondarily. Instead, according to scholars, Baum had written a political allegory designed to take the populist side in a debate that raged at the time over whether to back the US dollar by using silver or gold.

In the original story, I observed, Dorothy's slippers were silver and it was Hollywood that gave Judy Garland ruby red ones. When you knew that, then the connections that you usually make with an allegory matching images with realities begin to make sense: silver walks on the yellow (gold) brick road, symbolizing the proper relationship between the two metals. Dorothy is from drought-stricken Kansas and symbolizes those held hostage to the interests favoring gold. Struggling, she makes her way to Oz. "Oz," I pointed out, is the abbreviation for ounces, the measurement used to weigh gold, and the city, which symbolizes Washington, D.C., is green because that is the color of US currency.

In her quest to find a way home, Dorothy and the populists who favor silver are carried to this strange land by a tornado, symbolizing a victory at the polls. And Dorothy is assisted by her friends: the Tinman (northeastern factory workers), the Scarecrow (midwestern farmers), the Lion (William Jennings Bryan), and Glenda, the good witch of the west (voters from California). Together, I told them, Baum believed that populist forces could write a new day in US political history.

Isn't it telling that we could miss so much of the story's meaning in spite of the fact that *The Wizard of Oz* was written scarcely a century ago, in our own language and in our own country? If we could make that many mistakes, how many more would we make without the benefit of historical study, in trying to understand a book written over two millennia ago, in another language, in another culture, under circumstances about which we know infinitely less?

Such was my opening gambit in support of a historical-critical approach to the interpretation of John's Apocalypse. My students were always "wowed" by the illustration, if a bit distressed at the way in which I had ruined the Bible *and* a perfectly good children's story for them—all in one fell swoop.

The problem, it turns out, is that the scholars might have been wrong about *The Wizard of Oz*. Research over the last five years suggests that—far from populist in his leanings—Baum was, in fact, a republican and when on a rare occasion he commented on matters of a political nature he was almost always direct. So, it's hard to imagine that he made this argument and chose such an elaborate means of nailing his point. His own reflections on the composition of the book indicates that he had no intention of writing a political allegory, but was, in fact, completely enthralled with the prospect of entertaining young children.

Now, when I learned this, I was tempted to drop the illustration. After all, my students' childhood readings of the story were not all that different from what Baum evidently intended. But then it occurred to me that the same historical methods that had been used to argue that the story was a political allegory were also the methods that vindicated the reading of it as a children's story. In other words, if those who want to read John's Apocalypse without reference to history are consoled by the fact that a historian or two could be wrong about a book written in our language, in our own country, scarcely a century ago, they should also remember that it is the historical-critical method that has made the case for continuing to read *The Wizard of Oz* as a children's fairytale!

And herein lies the argument to be made for a historical-critical reading in preference to the roadmap approach. The intuitive approach that we all rightly take to reading is grounded in the question, "What did the writer mean or intend?" It is not always an easy question to answer and when asked about literature written in the distant past, it is a question that can only be answered with degrees of probability. But without some idea of the author's intended meaning, there is, in the final analysis, no means of knowing what a passage does or does not mean or of adjudicating between interpretations.

> *Without some idea of the author's intended meaning, there is, in the final analysis, no means of knowing what a passage does or does not mean or of adjudicating between interpretations.*

Roadmap-readings and mythic readings that are not grounded in questions about the author's intent are without that kind of accountability. In fact, the logic of a roadmap-reading flies in the face of that intuition, reasoning that the original author wrote about a vision that he did not comprehend for an audience that did not understand it, and only now, at long last—maybe!—will there be someone who can.

Continuing the Conversation . . .

For historical readings of John's Apocalypse, see David E. Aune, *Revelation: Word Biblical Commentary* (3 vols.; ed. Bruce M. Metzger; Dallas: Word Books, Publisher, 1997, 1998, 1998); Elisabeth Schüssler Fiorenza, *Revelation: Vision of a Just World* (Proclamation Commentaries; ed. Gerhard Krodel; Minneapolis: Fortress Press, 1991); Leonard L. Thompson, *The Book of Revelation: Apocalypse and Empire* (New York: Oxford University Press, 1990).

CHAPTER FOUR

A Deeper Reality: Revelation 1:1–5:14

Will those of you who live in Asia Minor, knowing the deeper nature of reality . . .

The Book of Revelation defies easy organization. There is no chronology. The word *plot* does not apply, although some scholars have tried to use it. The world disappears entirely in one scene and returns in another and some transitions in the action are left entirely unexplained, forcing roadmap interpreters to borrow freely from books centuries apart in order to create order where there is none. Even the much-used number seven cannot explain everything that the writer does. The most that one can say by way of outline is that John's vision has three movements that ask a single question: *Will those of you who live in Asia Minor, knowing the deeper nature of reality,* [movement one: 1:1–5:14] *time and the future,* [movement two: 6:1–16:21] *live your lives in the City of Babylon or the City of God* [movement three: 17:1–22:21]?[1]

As we go along, that is the outline I'll use to explore John's meaning. In each chapter we will also look at other issues that bear on the way that we read the Apocalypse. In this chapter, for example, we will look at the oral character of John's work, the nature of the crisis within the church of his day, the genre (or nature) of the literature John is using, and the way in which he uses it to change his readers' perceptions of reality.

John's Apocalypse and the Oral Mind

> So in America when the sun goes down and I sit on the old broken-down river pier watching the long, long skies over New Jersey and sense all that raw land that rolls in one unbelievable huge bulge over to the West Coast, and all that road going, all the people dreaming in the immensity of it, and in Iowa I know by now the children must be crying in the land where they let the children cry, and tonight the stars'll be out, and don't you know that God is Pooh Bear? the evening star must be drooping and shedding her sparkler dims on the prairie, which is just before the coming of complete night that blesses the earth, darkens all rivers, cups the peak and folds the final shore in, and nobody, nobody knows what's going to happen to anybody besides the forlorn rags of growing old, I think of Dean Moriarty, I even think of old Dean Moriarty, the father we never found, I think of Dean Moriarty.[2]

Have you ever noticed what a difference there is between reading a printed word and listening to something read out loud? The printed word can be read and re-read. We can take notes, scribble in the margins, and go back when we are not clear about what a writer is saying. It's an exercise that requires us to read and comprehend in specific ways, using what anthropologists sometimes call an "alphabetic mind." You and I are both using our alphabetic minds right now. I'm relying on mine to put words down on paper and to communicate a message. You are using yours to read and understand them. By contrast, when we listen to the written word read aloud we are using our "oral minds." The challenge to hear and understand words read aloud is completely different from the one required by the "alphabetic mind." You have to remember more and picture the words in your head. Large and long sentences are easily forgotten and there is nothing to go back and review.

You and I switch back and forth between the alphabetic and oral minds, though we rely heavily on the alphabetic part of our brains. But ancient cultures, like the one to which John wrote his Apocalypse, relied almost completely on their oral minds. In fact, because only a few people received the education needed to read and write, the oral mind was the only one that most people had an opportunity to develop. As a result, a small number of people did all of the reading and writing for everyone else, and most of what was written was written to be heard, not read.

> *A small number of people did all of the reading and writing for everyone else, and most of what was written was written to be heard, not read.*

That's what makes the passage from Jack Kerouac's book *On the Road*, which I've quoted above, such a great illustration of what John is trying to do in his Apocalypse. One of the leading "beat poets" of the 1940s and early 1950s, Kerouac was accustomed to reading his work out loud to his audiences. His ability to reach the oral mind was so deeply ingrained in his work that when he wrote something, he wrote to be heard. That's the case here. Read Kerouac's words out loud or, better yet, have someone read them to you. Do you hear the strategies he uses to paint a memorable, visual image?[3]

One strategy that Kerouac used is simply to add images to the verbal picture he is painting. Dependent clauses that provide explanations and qualify a statement that has been made can lose an audience. But add words and phrases over and over again, and you begin to communicate. In the brief passage that I've included here, Kerouac uses the conjunction "and" nine times, adding image to image, omitting any explanation of how the images are related or why he uses them.

But it's not enough to add images to the picture. They also need to build on one another. Complementary and overlapping images create an ever larger impression. Kerouac himself once told other writers to "build up words till satisfaction is gained" and ancient communicators would have agreed.[4] So he gives us pictures of New Jersey, the West Coast, and Iowa, creating a picture of a mind that ranges freely over America.

For that reason Kerouac's picture and oral communication in general is also marked by *redundant* images. People who listen to the spoken word rather than read it remember more of what they hear than those who are accustomed to reading. But they didn't remember what they heard simply because their memories were better or because they were more effective listeners—though they probably were. They also remembered more because the people who communicated with them repeated things over and over again.

All three of these oral strategies are used in the Book of Revelation, which was originally heard, not read. The writer relies from the very beginning on vivid imagery. Seven messages are sent to seven churches (Rev 2:1–3:22); seven beatitudes are pronounced in the course of the book as a whole (Rev 1:3; 14:13; 16:15; 19:9; 20:6: 22:7, 14); seven words of praise are spoken (Rev 5:12); seven kinds of people are described (Rev 6:15); seven references are made to the altar (Rev 6:9; 8:3, 5; 9:13; 11:1; 14:18; 16:7); the eschatological (or final) return of Christ is described seven times (Rev 2:16; 3:11; 16:15; 22:7, 12, 17, 20); seven seals, seven trumpets, and seven bowls serve as the centerpiece of the book's visions (Rev 6:1–18:24); and seven scenes describe God's triumph (Rev 19:11–22:20a).

Like the Beat poets of Kerouac's day, John seems to say, "You might think about this way—now this way—then this way." Additive, aggregative, redundant—the effort to systematize his vision is like trying to imagine the travel itinerary that allows Kerouac to see first New Jersey, then the West Coast, and now the plains of Iowa. It's not that Kerouac or John makes no sense. The effort itself is misplaced. Kerouac isn't writing a Michelin travel guide and John isn't drawing a roadmap. Revelation's public use and its appeal to the oral mind is named at the outset: "Blessed is the *one who reads aloud* the words of the prophecy, and blessed are *those who hear and who keep* what is written in it; for the time is near" (Rev 1:3; emphasis mine).

Here then, in a single sentence is the burden of the first movement. In our culture a blessing is an ephemeral thing, a means of expressing well-wishes, but hard to pin down either as to origins or its impact. For John, this blessing is far weightier. It's meant to sustain those who hear him in the midst of crisis and to shape their behavior.

Blessed is the one who reads aloud *the words of the prophecy, and blessed are* those who hear *and who* keep what is written in it; for the time is near. —REV 1:3

It is not a means of expressing well-*wishes*, but of conferring well-*being*. In our day words are powerful; they can secure an advantage and shape perceptions. In John's day, however, words had the power to change reality. They registered a fact and the fact registered here is that the blessing has already been given. The blessing rests upon the reader or lector and those who hear.

But for John, as for his Jewish forbearers, hearing—registering the fact that a word has been spoken—is not enough. Those who are blessed both hear and "keep" the word spoken. Truth is not just something given, but lived. In a time of crisis, the leisure of truth-discussed gives way to truth-that-must-be-lived. Fidelity is a public, observable matter. So, for John, the question becomes, can the churches hear? No analysis will do. This is a spoken word, not a written one. The question is one of will, not of capability. And the message is imaginative, vivid, and immediate.

So, for John, the question becomes, can the churches hear?

The glorified Christ, standing in the midst of seven golden lampstands, each representing one of the churches, appears before them, individually and as a community. He wears a long robe with a golden sash across his chest. His hair is as white as white wool or snow. His eyes are like a flame of fire, his feet like burnished bronze, and his voice like the sound of many waters.

There's no intermediary between the glorified Christ and his listeners either. The reason that the churches will need to weigh their response carefully is because this message comes from the Son of Man himself. He knows them intimately; he holds the stars that represent each of them in his hand.

The fact that each church is represented by an angel reflects an ancient and Jewish conviction that everything that takes place on earth is mirrored in the councils of God. This is not the same thing as the Greek notion of ideals or perfect versions of imperfect and earthly realities. It is, instead, a notion that touches instead on relational and moral categories and is deeply associated with the creative intention of God.

In ancient Israel the Temple and the priesthood stood at the nexus of this connection. The Temple and its priesthood were, at the risk of oversimplification, devoted to cosmic housekeeping. Purity had little to do with things being clean and had far more to do with things serving the purpose that God intended for them. Defilement had little to do with being dirty and far more to do with being misused. There was a place for everything and everything should be in its place. When it was not, rituals and sacrifices set things right.

So, as the glorified Christ addresses the angels representing each church, John signals that the choices being made by the members of each congregation are momentous. These are not trivial choices, but choices that reverberate throughout the fabric of heaven and earth. John is about to sketch those choices in cosmic terms, but for now it is important for his hearers to know that the choices they make are of enormous consequence.

John knows his audience well. They identify strongly with their Jewish roots. They believe themselves to represent the true Israel and they would have recognized the symbolism for Israel that comes from Zechariah's image of a seven-branched candelabra. They would have also recognized the image of Christ standing in the heavenly council, where everything that happens on earth has its counterpart in heaven, including the stars that represent angels assigned to each of the seven churches.

But this image does not simply authorize the message or give us some sense of where each of the churches fit in the divine economy. It also underlines the fact that Christ is present among the churches *now*. This is why no theology or even an eschatology that is preoccupied with the future will ever accurately represent the spirituality of John's Apocalypse. The Christ who will come again is already present. So real is that presence that some scholars have suggested that the prescript (or formal introduction) to the letters may, in fact, have been cast in the form of a responsive reading designed to be used in a worship service:

Lector:
Grace to you and peace from him who is and who was
and who is to come,
and from the seven spirits who are before his throne,
and from Jesus Christ the faithful witness,
The firstborn of the dead, and the ruler of the kings of the earth.

Assembly:
To him who loves us
and freed us from our sins by his blood,
and made us a kingdom, priests serving his God and Father,
to him be glory and dominion for ever and ever. Amen.

Lector:

> Look, he is coming with the clouds;
> every eye will see him,
> even those who pierced him;
> and on his account all tribes of the earth will wail.

Assembly:

> So it is to be. Amen.

Lector:

> I am the Alpha and the Omega,
> says the Lord God,
> who is and who was and who is to come,
> the Almighty.[5]

The Crisis within the Church

The original recipients were no doubt alive to the symbolic—even mythic—character of John's seven letters to the seven churches (Rev 2:1–3:22). They bear far too much similarity to one another to have been written on separate occasions.

- Each one is addressed to an angel that represents a church.
- Each church is located in a major city.
- Each letter contains the prophetic formula, "Thus says the Lord . . ."
- The writer attributes a characteristic to the glorified Christ in each pronouncement.
- The knowledge of Christ is affirmed: "I know . . ."
- The body of the letter contains "praise and/or blame, promise, and/or threat."
- Each contains a call to "hear."
- And those who conquer are promised a blessing.

In addition, the content of the letters follows a pattern, moving from censure and commendation of the church in Ephesus; to praise of Smyrna, Thyatira, and Philadelphia; to censure in the case of Pergamum, Sardis, and Laodicea. As such, at one level the letters should be understood as a single message, not seven. The multiplication of letters appeals to the oral mind. The redundant features underline again and again the same point and the number seven symbolizes completion and, therefore, probably alludes to the providential balance of God at work in the world.

But John's congregations would have been alive to the specifics of the debate within their churches as well. Located in major urban areas along the same highway in western Asia Minor, the churches were each roughly thirty to forty miles apart and, following the destruction of Jerusalem in 70 CE, they were at the heart of both the life of the church and the life of the Roman Empire. All seven cities had Roman courts in which Christians might have been tried. At least three, if not more, had temples dedicated to Caesar (Ephesus, Smyrna, and Pergamum).

So the letters move between the mythic and representational on the one hand and the mundane or the particular on the other hand. For that reason, the attributes and shortcomings attributed to each of the churches are less important on a church-by-church basis than they are for the patterns that emerge. John's original audience might have taken to heart the description of their individual congregations, but heard together, they would have also known that the descriptions were representative of the church as a whole. None of the individual congregations were probably as uniformly "good" or "bad" as John's descriptions might seem to suggest at first blush.

One of the patterns that contemporary readers usually observe immediately is the implied tension between the church and the world around it. Roadmap-readings have prepared us to believe that John's church was deeply alienated and lived in a society that was profoundly hostile, and certainly, there is evidence of that alienation.

One of the patterns that contemporary readers usually observe immediately is the implied tension between the church and the world around it.

Like Paul's churches, consuming meat sacrificed to idols appears to have been an issue and the struggle between the "weak" (who objected to eating it) and the "strong" (who did not) seems to have been a problem (Rev 2:14, 2:20). A second issue appears to have been philosophical speculation of some kind and may have involved Christians who entertained the kind of ideas that would much later be identified with what we know today as Gnosticism, although it is very hard to know (Rev 2:20, 23, 24).

But read carefully with an ear to the original situation and it is clear that a description of that kind is far too simple to be satisfactory. For one thing, to the extent that the church did live in tension with the world around it, those tensions clearly had two centers, not just one. Conflict with Rome and Roman culture was a factor and that conflict looms even larger later in the Apocalypse. But here, alongside that emphasis, is also evidence of a painful struggle with the Judaism of the day. References to the synagogue of Satan (Rev 2:9, 3:9) suggest that the widespread expulsion of Christians from the worship of which they were fully a part was a source of no small pain to the churches of Asia Minor and some no doubt struggled to maintain their relationship with the Jewish community.

> **Gnosticism:** a loosely organized movement in early Christianity that believed we make spiritual progress by acquiring *gnosis,* or secret knowledge; the Gnostics believed the material world was inherently evil, the spiritual world inherently good.

It is anachronistic, however, to talk in terms of anti-Semitism. As they experienced it, this was for John's congregations an *intra*-religious and *intra*-Jewish conflict—a conflict between Jews—not a struggle between Jews and Christians. This is why John uses the image of the New Jerusalem (Rev 3:12), which he will develop at greater length. When he castigates the behavior of others, he draws on the lore of ancient Judaism, calling them Balaam (Rev 2:14) and Jezebel (Rev 2:20f.), just as Jews had always drawn on the infamous figures in their history to caricature one another in times of conflict. The debate is not about Christianity's right of succession, it is debate about how one's Jewishness is best expressed.

What is even more striking about the crisis described in these letters, however, is the way in which the situation *within* the church looms far larger than the conflict with either Rome or the synagogue. It is here that John focuses; it is with the church in mind as its primary audience that he writes his Apocalypse; and it is the church's relationship to the dominant culture that lies at the heart of John's concern.

Competing Perceptions

John's churches were probably comparable in character to the churches to which Paul had ministered. They were located in urban centers. Their membership probably varied widely in educational background, and they no doubt differed greatly in socioeconomic terms. In many cases, however, they probably achieved a social status that brought them into contact with the Roman mainstream.

This placed John's followers in no small measure of tension with the culture of which they were a part, and John plainly believed that the choices they faced were stark ones fraught with spiritual peril. But it would be a mistake to assume that the issues they faced presented themselves as a simple and obvious choice between the God of their own faith and that of the religions around them. Personal relationships, shared economic interests, and the desire for a certain measure of status within the community probably generated a variety of reactions. While John's followers were probably conscious of some tensions, others either completely escaped their notice or led them to conclude that there was no necessary difficulty.

And, in fact, a careful reading of the letters suggests that not all of John's congregations shared his concerns. This, for example, is clearly the implication of John's words to the church in Laodicea to which he writes: "I know your works; you are neither cold nor hot. I wish that you were either cold or hot. So, because you are lukewarm, and neither cold nor hot, I am about to spit you out of my mouth" (Rev 3:15–16).

"I know your affliction and your poverty, even though you are rich. I know the slander on the part of those who say that they are Jews and are not, but are a synagogue of Satan." —REV 2:9

Typically, the popular interpretation of this passage grasps the general sense of John's meaning. Christ is grieved by the church's "lukewarm" or indifferent mindset. But in referring to hot and cold water, the meaning is not to be understood as "I wish you were devoted to God (hot) or hostile to the Gospel (cold)." John is probably referring to both the hot and cold medicinal waters that were so popular in nearby Hierapolis and Colossae at the time. So, instead, both are positive metaphors with which lukewarm or tepid water is contrasted as worthless.

In other words, John is saying, "I wish you were hot or cold redemptive water, but since you are lukewarm, Christ will spew you from his mouth." This observation combined with the sharp references to wealth and self-sufficiency in the letter to the Laodiceans suggests that, from John's point of view, they had remained indifferent to the issues that had split other congregations.

It would be dangerous to assume that in every case such variations in the response of John's congregations to the culture around them corresponded directly to differences in wealth, education, and social status. In spite of John's blanket condemnation of the church in Laodicea, it is difficult to imagine that every member of even that community responded in precisely the same way to questions of Christian practice. But granted the inevitable exceptions, the fact remains that those who live on "high street" and those who live on "main street" (to use a modern metaphor) really do see the choices between Christ and culture in very different ways.

The fact remains that those who live on "high street" and those who live on "main street" really do see the choices between Christ and culture in very different ways.

A Question of Identity

Exactly how any of us would evaluate the choices that John and his churches faced is difficult to say. The limited amount of information available to us and the radically different perspectives that we would bring to the situation make a question of that kind all but pointless. But clearly imbedded in the choices that prompted John to write is the question of Christian identity.

Will you live your lives according to the dictates of the culture or of Christ?

By prompting his readers to think of themselves as standing among the seven lamps in the presence of the glorified Christ, John challenges the churches of Asia Minor to begin considering a radical or root issue that he will go on to develop: will you live your lives according to the dictates of the culture or of Christ?

This will never be an easy question to answer and our response will always be shaped to some extent by our social location and personal experience. But if there is a question arising out of John's seven letters to the seven churches of Asia Minor that we need to answer and can, that is probably one that requires our attention.

Defining a Genre: Apocalyptic Literature

I frequently drive past a church marquee with a space on the sign to advertise a program or offer a word of wisdom. On balance, I think that those signs are a mistake. As a rule, any theology that you find on a sign or a bumper sticker is almost always far too short to be of any value and a great deal of it is very dangerous.

Not long ago, driving home one evening, the same sign offered a bit of biblical interpretation: "God has called us to be fishers of men. You catch 'em, God will clean 'em." Images of God cleaning a human being in the same way that one might clean or scale a fish immediately came to mind and I wondered: did the people who offered that bit of advice realize that they had pressed the parable beyond its point of comparison, trying to make it do work that it was never intended to do?

The same kinds of questions are the ones to ask when reading the Bible. To know something about the *genre* or type of literature that a writer is using is of enormous value; it frames our expectations as we read and provides an important clue to the meaning of what we are reading. To know that a love letter and a refrigerator guarantee are two different kinds of literature is very important—both for lovers and for the refrigerator manufacturers. The same is true of John's Apocalypse. Knowing that it is apocalyptic literature helps us know what John is trying to communicate.

Saying everything that might be said about apocalyptic literature in the space available to us would be both impossible and beside the point here. Among the apocalyptic literature preserved from the ancient world are pieces that amount to little more than imaginative tours of heaven and hell while others, like the Book of Revelation, are clearly grounded in a historical experience and a religious crisis. The word *apocalypse* means an "unveiling" or "uncovering," but ancient apocalyptic literature varies so greatly that you can put just so much weight on the etymology (or origin) of the word itself.

Knowing this, scholars have tried to be more precise by identifying the characteristics that appear in apocalyptic literature. One such list, for example, posits that apocalyptic literature includes:

- discourse cycles (conversations between heavenly messengers or God and the writer)
- spiritual turmoils (the fear or dismay that follows seeing the future, for example)
- paraenetic discourses (ethical injunctions given in light of what has been heard)

- pseudonymity (the writer's use of an assumed name—often someone famous from the past)
- mythical images rich in symbolism (we talked about these in chapter 2)
- composite character (use of more than one kind of literature within the apocalypse—John's use of letters, for example)
- urgent expectation of the end, cosmic catastrophe
- world history divided into segments
- angels and demons
- promise of salvation
- the throne of God
- a mediator with royal functions and
- frequent use of the word glory[6]

This is not a bad list, but not every apocalypse has all of these elements. The Book of Revelation, for example, contains a number of characteristics identified above, but not all. There is little or no evidence to suggest that the writer was using a pseudonym or assumed name. His name probably was John, we just don't know which one, and he doesn't make enough of the apostolic connection with the John of the same name to suggest that he intended that association.

Because the characteristics of an apocalypse can vary in this way, other scholars have attempted to develop definitions that contain only the elements that are essential to the nature of apocalyptic literature. One scholar, for example, identifies an apocalypse as a narrative (or story) in which an otherworldy mediator (an angel, for example) discloses a transcendent reality (i.e., a reality beyond normal human knowledge) that is both temporal (i.e., deals with human experience, past and present) and spatial (i.e., reveals something about heaven and/or hell).[7] As definitions go, this is certainly one of the best, but it is unlikely that this effort represents the last word on the subject.

In part, that is because defining a *genre* or type of literature isn't a prescriptive task. We're not laying down rules that writers must follow, nor are we trying to discover the rules that they were given, since there weren't any hard and fast rules. Instead, what these scholars are attempting is a descriptive task in which they try to say something about the way in which a roughly similar kind of literary work is used by a number of different authors writing at different times and in different places. So the labels are of enormous value, but they will slip and blur at the edges as writers exercise their freedom to use a particular literary medium and as the needs they address vary from place to place. For our purposes, then, it works well to sit lightly between the definition on the one hand and the list on the other. This approach will orient us in general terms to the nature of apocalyptic literature without tying us to an overly specific set of criteria.

If I were going to tailor a definition to capture both the nature of apocalyptic literature and the creative use that John makes of it, I might apply and modify the definition given above in this way:

> John seeks to unveil or uncover what he considers to be the deeper realities about both time and the world in which the churches of Asia Minor live. He does this by taking his hearers on an imaginative tour of both the divine throne room (or council) and the future. In so doing he hopes to change his hearers' perceptions of the present and, in particular, the nature of the spiritual crisis that they face. His ultimate goal is to encourage those who share his views and persuade those who do not to embrace his views, shaping not just their beliefs, but their lives.

In the remainder of this chapter I want to look at two of the elements above: uncovering deeper realities, and John's use of the throne room and the world, as they apply to Rev 4:1–5:14.

Uncovering Deeper Realities

Some apocalyptic literature has a genuinely speculative nature and explores arcane secrets about heaven, hell, and time and has no immediate or obvious bearing on the hearer's understanding of life. It has, instead, the feel of an imaginative or intellectual exercise. Whether that, in fact, is entirely fair to such literature is not at all clear. Given the fragmentary character of some of the literature left to us, it may well be that the clues to the writer's interests have been lost. Factor in the antiquity of that literature and the difficulties associated with recovering its historical context, and it is difficult to know exactly what prompted some writers to compose an apocalypse.

But in John's case deeper realities—or, one might say, the true nature of the choices facing the church—are at the heart of his concerns. He is, as we have seen, keenly aware that there are those in the churches of Asia Minor who are all but unaware of what he considers a momentous threat to their spiritual well-being. He is also aware that he has active opponents in those churches who interpret the tensions between Christ and culture in very different terms.

John undoubtedly had little or no hope of changing the views of the people he describes as Jezebel and Balaam: the epithets he uses to describe them make that clear. But his whole reason for writing the Apocalypse lies in influencing the behavior of the people worshipping in those churches.

Studies of comparative religious ethics state that in reinforcing any prescriptive demand, the person making the demand must find a way of justifying it. They may not always be articulated in a systematic fashion but it is always implied. In making a demand, for example, a religious leader might appeal to a sanction for failing to respond, or to rules and principles that are shared by the community. But the ultimate appeal—and the one that usually surfaces alongside the others—is an appeal to authority and in the case of religious demands, that authority is usually the authority of God. An appeal to divine authority lends superiority and legitimacy to the demands that one might make that almost no other appeal can provide. Even the prospect of judgment for the sins we might commit means very little to us if we do not believe in the authority behind the demand. The appeal to divine authority is, for that reason, the most basic of all appeals.

This is why John is preoccupied with the teachers he calls Balaam and Jezebel. This is why he uses derogatory terms to describe them, attacking both the superiority and legitimacy of their claims. And that is why, at the beginning of this section of the Apocalypse (Rev 4:1)— as at the beginning of the seven letters to the seven churches (Rev 1:19)—it is the resurrected and glorified Christ, not John, who speaks.[8]

The initial scene in the throne room or divine council is described in terms that parody the throne room of the imperial court of the Caesars. By using imagery from Deuteronomy and Leviticus that is associated with the Temple, John's description of the divine voice that he hears claims ascendancy and, therefore, authority over the messages of both Rome and the synagogue.

Then I turned to see whose voice it was that spoke to me, and on turning I saw seven golden lampstands, and in the midst of the lampstands I saw one like the Son of Man, clothed with a long robe and with a golden sash across his chest. —REV 1:12–13

But the description of the divine voice is thoroughly Christological—that is, associated with the person and work of Christ. So the divine voice that the churches hear is one to which they would be inclined to assign greater weight. The open door of heaven, the voice like a trumpet, and the invitation to "come up" all usher the hearer into the presence of Christ, and this encounter becomes the means by which John imaginatively redefines the way in which his audience sees life's realities.

The Throne Room and the World

In defining this reality the tour of the divine throne room or council plays an important part in shaping the experience of John's hearers, couching all that they are about to hear and thereby see in the triumph and worship of the resurrected Christ. So, in a world occupied by would-be rulers and temporal thrones, John focuses the hearer's attention on the throne of Christ, using the word "throne" forty-seven of the sixty-two times that it appears in the New Testament.

John lived in a world in which the cosmic and the earthly are thought to be closely related and in which the claims to divinity rested far more frequently on the ability to order the world, rather than account for its existence. So John begins his vision by making it clear that the divine throne *is* occupied—and *not* by the emperor Domitian. To underline his point the initial throne room scene is filled with allusions to the claims to divinity and ceremony that would have attended the *adventus* or arrival of the emperor as he traveled from city to city, dispensing justice, hearing petitions, and receiving embassies. For example:

- Domitian demanded, or was often greeted, using the title *dominus et deus* (Lord and God). That greeting is echoed in the words of the "four living creatures" who attend Christ's throne (Rev 4:8).
- The acclamation that attended the emperor's triumphal entry is reflected in the acclamation of the Son in Rev 5:9: "You are worthy."

- The twenty-four elders who "fall before the one who is seated on the throne" (*proskynesis,* or prostration) and who throw their crowns down in front of his throne, mimic the behavior of the lictors (or officers) who accompany the emperor and who carried the symbols of his authority (Rev 4:9–11).
- And the elders, like the rainbow (Rev 4:3) and, at other times, the angels (Rev 5:11; 7:11), encircle the divine throne, representing the whole of the cosmos, of which the resurrected Christ is the *axis mundi* or the center around which all else revolves (Rev 4:4). Their white robes represent both purity and victory, but unlike their Roman counterparts, the crowns that they offer are gold: a far more precious gift, suggesting perhaps the higher esteem, devotion, and authority that Christ deserves.
- Even the hymns sung before Christ's throne parody the hymns written in honor of the emperor and imperial pretensions to divinity (Rev 4:8, 11; 5:9–10, 12–13).

Placing his vision of the throne room or divine council first, John's message is clear: the churches can only understand the nature of all the other realities that he is about to unveil, if they understand this reality: Christ, emperor, rules over all.

Aware of the tensions presented by the church's relationship with the synagogues of Asia Minor, using images from the Hebrew Bible that were familiar to his listeners was both a natural and rhetorically strategic dimension of John's vision.

- The throne image itself harkens back to the throne-chariot of Ezekiel (Ezek 1:4–28).
- The references to "flashes of lightning" and "peals of thunder" (Rev 4:5) were associated with prophetic visions (Ps 77:17–18; Ezek 1:4, 13, 14, 24) and Moses' encounter with God on Sinai (Exod 19:16).
- The reference to a sea of glass before the throne (Rev 4:6) alludes to the chaotic waters at the beginning of creation (Gen 1:1–10); and the fact that they are described as crystalline suggests that they have been conquered.
- Even the throne room itself is replete with angelic visitors (Rev 4:6–11) that are described as having attended the throne of the God in Jewish tradition (Ezek 1 and Isa 6).

John may have taken considerable pains to paint an image of a throne occupied by Christ in contradiction to the claims of the emperor. But he is also anxious to underline the continuity between Israel and the church. No claim to authority for his message would have made sense without it and neither John nor his audience could have imagined a different wellspring for the images of divine rule used here.

> The churches can only understand the nature of all the other realities that he is about to unveil, if they understand this reality: Christ, emperor, rules over all.

This emphasis on continuity with Jewish tradition is all the more important because alongside the more conventional images from the Hebrew Bible associated with the throne of God, John then introduces a completely new emphasis that he will return to over and over again, announcing that the one he sees on the throne is the Lamb (Rev 5:6). Juxtaposed with the earlier announcement that it is the Lion of Judah (aka, the King) who sits on the throne (Rev 5:5), John underlines the comparisons to be made between the two, moving from God the Father to God the Son and from images of God's sovereignty over creation to an emphasis on God's sovereignty over the re-creation made possible through the suffering of the Lamb.

The image of the Lamb conjures up associations with the Passover feast, deliverance of Israel's children from slavery in Egypt, and the sacrifice made by the crucified Christ on behalf of the church. But the main point seems to be that the one who sits on the throne conquers by dying. The point could not have been lost on John's congregations: The one who really sits on the throne has experienced the same rejection that they have

> At once I was in the spirit, and there in heaven stood a throne, with one seated on the throne! —REV 4:2

and the Lamb will acquit them, even if the Roman courts do not. It is clear, then, that John has more in mind than the issue of authority. Sanctions (or incentives) play an important role as well.

Exactly what John's hearers would have heard is harder to say. The complex images that he uses would have refracted like light through a prism, varying in color and hue depending upon the religious and social location of the one doing the hearing. Certainly John hoped to reassure some in the communities to which he wrote; and those who agreed with him no doubt saw the crystalline character of the waters by the throne of Christ as a powerful counterpoint to the chaos that marked their lives. Likewise the realization that their weakness—like that of the Lamb—was not a fatal flaw would also be a source of encouragement. Others, he no doubt hoped, would feel convicted and moved by what they heard, hearing and thereby seeing the choice set before them as an invitation to stand among the twenty-four elders or to withdraw from their circle.

> Then I saw between the throne and the four living creatures and among the elders a Lamb standing as if it had been slaughtered, having seven horns and seven eyes, which are the seven spirits of God sent out into all the earth. —REV 5:6

How the churches actually reacted was, naturally, another matter. On one end of the spectrum there were surely those who felt as smug as they did reassured. On the other end of the spectrum there were those who were probably offended by John's message and believed that the concessions they made to the culture around them were all but trivial. From John's point of view, however, he had alerted his readers to the deeper realities behind the choices they would make and he was now ready to describe the future and one of two cities with which they might choose to ally themselves.

Two Horizons

On the face of it, biblical scholars may seem preoccupied with the past, but much of the work done on the biblical text is, in fact, done with a view to probing the significance of Scripture for the lives of its contemporary readers. Moving, of course, from the text to our lives without co-opting Scripture to make it say what we would like for it to say, or without glossing over the considerable differences between our world and the world of the text, is the challenge. For that reason, many scholars talk about the two horizons between which contemporary readers move: the horizon of the original readers and writers—their world, their concerns, their views—and our horizon—our world, our concerns, and our views.

We interpret Scripture most effectively when, to the best of our ability, we understand the text's meaning as fully as possible. This occurs when we allow the horizon of the world in which its original writer and readers lived to inform the way in which we interpret the text. We avoid putting words in the author's mouth. We try not to bend and distort the writer's meaning. We are aware that the task of

Moving from the text to our lives without co-opting Scripture to make it say what we would like for it to say, or without glossing over the considerable differences between our world and the world of the text, is the challenge.

interpretation means attending very carefully to the horizon from which the text came.

We apply Scripture best, then, when having done this interpretive work, we consider what that effort will and will not permit us to assume that Scripture says. Of course, what follows is the difficult task of deciding where and how that message speaks to our own horizon. The differences between our horizon and the horizon of the text may be so great that the point of application disappears completely or surfaces in an entirely new way. It makes little sense to describe those points of application in too much detail here, since even our own horizon can vary from person to person and culture to culture. But based on the material that we have discussed thus far, we can make some observations that have implications for our own lives and for the way in which we read the Book of Revelation.

- The oral strategies that John uses emphasize that his Apocalypse is not speculative in nature. Far from interested in imagining what heaven is like, he is, instead, interested in the deeper reality behind the world in which he and the churches of Asia Minor live.
- For John the deeper nature of that reality has been masked by the lure of the emperor's city. He makes his point using apocalyptic literature as a means of picturing in vivid terms the deeper reality to which his churches owe their attention. It is not the reality of this world, but the reality reflected in the throne room of God where all the genuinely decisive decisions have already been made by God.
- The only ones in the churches of Asia Minor who can claim God's blessing are those who heed the words of the resurrected and glorified Christ.
- This doesn't mean that the church can escape all harm. A divine blessing does not carry immunity with it. John clearly believes that, in fact, the faithful may well face more than their fair share of misery. But he is also clear that the only benediction on their lives that matters is the benediction that God gives.

- So, for that reason, John portrays his words to the church as those of the exalted Christ who stands among the churches of Asia Minor, speaking directly to each of them. The churches may be tempted to believe that the choices they make are inconsequential, but they are marked by the deepest possible significance.
- He writes to the church about the fate of the church, not about the fate of those outside it.

In reading Revelation, then, it is clear that John did not write to answer some of the questions that we might raise today, living as we do with a very different horizon. The Apocalypse was not written to answer questions about the nature of heaven or the fate of those who are not Christians. It was written to the church about life in the church. It was also written to suggest that a deeper reality lies behind the choices that we make and that those choices are laden with significance for the shape of our relationship with God. The description of the throne room as well as the words of rebuke and encouragement spoken to the church by the exalted Christ are not described with a view to outlining the nature of divine judgment, nor as a means of describing the kind of behavior that will incur God's wrath or favor. The descriptions are, instead, meant to encourage the readers to look through this world to the reality that matters.

This, it seems to me, speaks directly to our lives. The tensions posed for us by the demands that this world makes upon us and the need to live with a view to the deeper reality of our lives in Christ change shape but never disappear. Just where, when, and how those tensions surface will always be a matter of debate, just as it was between John and his churches. What is important for us to acknowledge is that the tensions exist and that our status as the children of God requires that we grapple with the challenge those tensions pose for us. A meaningful conversation with Scripture in our day might grapple with the two issues that surface in John's own description of that struggle: the question of what is essential to a Christian identity shaped by that deeper reality, and the struggle to discern

> The tensions posed for us by the demands that this world makes upon us and the need to live with a view to the deeper reality in Christ change shape but never disappear.

clearly what is lost and gained in the accommodation that we all make to the cultures around us.

Continuing the Conversation . . .

For introductions to the Book of Revelation, see Judith Kovacs and Christopher Rowland, *Revelation: The Apocalypse of Jesus Christ* (Blackwell Bible Commentaries; ed. John Sawyer et al.; Oxford: Blackwell Publishing, 2004); Arthur W. Wainwright, *Mysterious Apocalypse: Interpreting the Book of Revelation* (Nashville: Abingdon Press, 1993); Craig R. Koester, *Revelation and the End of All Things* (Grand Rapids: Eerdmans, 2001).

For samples of other apocalyptic literature (both Jewish and Christian, biblical and extra-biblical), see Mitchell G. Reddish, ed., *Apocalyptic Literature: A Reader* (Nashville: Abingdon Press, 1990).

On the character of apocalyptic literature, see John J. Collins, *The Apocalyptic Imagination: An Introduction to the Jewish Matrix of Christianity* (New York: Crossroad, 1984); Paul D. Hanson, *The Dawn of Apocalyptic: The Historical and Sociological Roots of Jewish Apocalyptic Eschatology* (rev. ed.; Philadelphia: Fortress Press, 1979); Klaus Koch, *The Rediscovery of Apocalyptic* (trans. Margaret Kohl; London: SCM Press, 1972); Christopher Rowland, *The Open Heaven: A Study of Apocalyptic in Judaism and Early Christianity* (New York: Crossroads, 1982).

CHAPTER FIVE

A Different Kind of Time: Revelation 6:1–16:21

Time and the future . . .

The power we have to shape perceptions of time and the power those perceptions have in shaping our lives is something we rarely notice or acknowledge. Naively we assume that time is absolute and measurable. But that assumption isn't rooted in fact. It is rooted in the place that time occupies as part of what anthropologists call "primary level," or "core" culture.

"Primary" or "core" culture concepts are the standard furnishings of our lives. We take them for granted. They shape the way in which we evaluate the world around us. They are the "givens" of life. Like the ground under our feet and the sky over our heads, it requires a conscious effort to notice them and even more effort to realize that not only are there serious differences between cultures, but serious differences between individuals as well.

The very way in which we use the conception of time hints at our own culture's ability to manipulate and create alternative understandings of time—in spite of its apparent "givenness." When we fly from continent to continent we talk about jet lag, time zones, and biological time. When we attend university, we subdivide the day into class hours, measuring the amount of time devoted to lectures and (in some countries) the number of hours spent in class on a weekly basis. And from country to country we talk about the measure of precision that each of us expects, depending upon our cultural point of reference. Even the concept of timeliness is a cultural construct.

Religious literature has its own means of creating understandings of time as well, and the purely chronological or measurable is often of little or no relevance in such literature. In John's Apocalypse, for instance, the experience of hearing his vision read aloud transports the audience into a moment in which the present is decisively shaped by the future. The expectations of God and the promised deliverance of the church reshape the religious and ethical priorities of that moment. And while the hearers clearly expect a public and decisive deliverance to occur in the near future, the fulfillment of that promise doesn't matter nearly as much as the way in which the present has been radically redefined. While John continues to describe the deeper realities that the church faces, it is this redefinition of time and the future that looms ever larger at this point in his Apocalypse.

Time and the Future

In dealing with time and the future, the vision of eschatological woes that John reports are organized in three sets of seven. At the heart of each set is a specific image: seven seals (Rev 6:1–8:1), seven trumpets (Rev 8:6–11:19), and seven bowls (Rev 15:5–16:21). The trumpets begin with the opening of the seventh seal and the pattern of seven is more easily recognized in both the description of the seals and the trumpets, but the basic structure is the same throughout.

That said, the material does not follow seamlessly. John digresses from time to time and the victory of God's people is anticipated on a regular basis (Rev 7:1–17; 14:1–5; 15:2–4), probably for rhetorical and theological reasons.[1] He also comes back to the themes underlined in both the seven letters and the throne room vision, being careful not to lose track of the concerns that he has already raised. And between the visions surfaced by the trumpets and the bowls, John introduces an extended vision that transports the hearers to a mythic picture of the struggle he foresees for the church (Rev 12:1–14:20). After introducing all three sets of seven, he then unravels the significance of what he has described for the city of Babylon, aka Rome (Rev 17:1–18:24).

This approach underlines John's lack of interest in time as chronology. The overlapping and unreconciled character of the images lacks the kind of careful attention to order that one expects from someone who is concerned with time. A brief overview of each section demonstrates that, whatever John would like to accomplish, he has little or no interest in providing his readers with a timetable for his own day, much less for ours.

THE SEALS

The seven seals that keep the scroll closed in the first set of visions is a reference to the wax seals used to safeguard the contents of letters and other forms of communication in the ancient world. Opened only by the worthy Lamb, the image of the seal stresses the divine authority by which the scroll is secured and even where the Lamb is not the actor, it is the sovereign activity of Christ that is stressed again and again. As each seal is broken not only are the contents made public but events are set into motion. The image is no doubt borrowed from Ezek 2:9–3:3, where a similar scroll forecasts the judgment that is about to befall Jerusalem The resulting "eschatological woes" are described in great detail, seal by seal. But borrowing as John does from both myth and history, there is no firm distinction between events that have transpired, those that will be repeated, and those that will take place at some point in the future.

The first four seals are represented by riders astride horses and demonstrate the impact of war. Roughly speaking they are:

- conquest itself (Rev 6:1–2)
- the disappearance of peace (Rev 6:3–4)
- the economic dislocation that accompanies war and famine (Rev 6:5–6)
- and the resulting impact on the natural order, including disease and attacks by wild animals (Rev 6:7–8)

But the four are clearly meant to create a larger visual picture of the ravages of war as well as the coming judgment on Rome and should be read as such.

Then I saw the Lamb open one of the seven seals, and I heard one of the four living creatures call out, as with a voice of thunder, "Come!"
—REV 6:1

So, in one sense, the riders and their horses are mythic images and one might consign their activities completely to the future. But the image clearly alludes to the Parthian cavalry that successfully repelled the Romans in 62 CE and raised serious doubts about Roman supremacy. So it is impossible to distinguish between encounters that may have already troubled the Empire, the specter of future incursions by the Parthians, and the evocative character of the image that trades on the reality without being firmly tied to it.

The fifth seal draws the hearers' attention heavenward where the martyrs cry out "How long?" from beneath a heavenly altar and implore God for vengeance (Rev 6:9–11). John appears to be drawing here on Jewish tradition that the blood of martyrs was shed as a sacrifice and that the souls of the righteous found repose beneath the altar. He clearly believes that the martyrs will receive an answer. But the emphasis on the cry "how long?" raises very real questions about what, if any, assurances the hearers have about the timing of a divine intervention.

In response, the sixth seal unleashes cosmic havoc in which the stars fall from heaven; the sky is rolled up like a scroll; and mountains as well as islands are dislodged from their accustomed places (Rev 6:12–17). It is with this disaster that the sixth seal ends and the picture suggests that we have reached the earth's end as well. But as happens so often in the Apocalypse, the cosmos and earth will be back. It is clear that John believes the coming judgment will be universal and visible, but the end isn't the end.

Then, as is the case in both this set of seven images and the next, an interlude appears between the sixth and seventh seals (Rev 7:1–8). The interlude is significant. A representative 144,000 are sealed by God, not as a guarantee against suffering, but as an assurance of divine care. They are sealed here because with the breaking of the seventh and final seal, seven trumpets (echoing the plagues to which Egypt was subjected in Moses' day) will arrive. So, like the children of Israel, the churches of Asia Minor are reassured of God's presence with them. There are 144,000 because to ancient ears that number would have seemed incredibly large and to Jewish-Christian ears it would have also sounded complete (12 tribes of Israel × 12 disciples of Jesus = 144). But the theological motives for putting the interlude here is obviously what dominates the narrative and not a chronology.

When the final seal is opened, silence follows (Rev 8:1–5). John may be alluding to the silence urged at the dawn of judgment as in Zephaniah 1:3. Or perhaps the silence indicates the indeterminate character of that final judgment. But as John has made clear, what has transpired is either at God's urging or has transpired with God's permission and, through it all, the well-being of the church is secure. The prayers of the church rise like incense to the throne of God; John's readers are again brought in touch with the transcendent realities that lie behind the eschatological woes that they are about to see (Rev 8:1–5). Then, the first of seven trumpets are sounded (Rev 8:6f.).

> When the Lamb opened the seventh seal, there was silence in heaven for about half an hour. —REV 8:1

THE TRUMPETS

The trumpets, like the seals, integrate the kaleidoscopic vision that John is about to unveil. In ancient Israel trumpets were used in worship. But like the seals, they invite a variety of associations that also serve John's purpose: they are used to sound the beginning of battle, warning and victory, the enthronement of the king, and the eschatological day of the Lord.

The trumpets, however, don't announce the beginning of a new sequence of events that follow on those that are described by the opening of the scroll and the breaking of the seals. Patterned on the plagues that visited Egypt,[2] they describe the events that were outlined in the last sequence, but in even more vivid detail. A larger portion of the earth's population perishes in the coming judgment. The description that John offers describes not just the fall of Egypt, but all of history's tyrants who have ruled over the children of God.

In addition, the destruction now takes on a thoroughly cosmic dimension, affecting the land (Rev 8:7), sea (Rev 8:8–9), rivers (Rev 8:10–11), and heavens (Rev 8:12). New creatures call attention to the same emphasis on cosmic dislocation: an eagle circles over the earth announcing "woe" to its inhabitants (Rev 8:13). The locustlike creatures that attack possess the face of men, women's hair, the teeth of lions, chests like breastplates, wings that make the noise created by chariots, and the tails of scorpions (Rev 9:7–10). There are riders again, as well, but this time they are astride horses with tails like snakes poised to strike (Rev 9:19).

With the first trumpet, John foresees hail, fire, and blood cast upon the earth and a conflagration that consumes one third of the earth, its trees, and grass (Rev 8:7). With the second, a great mountain on fire is cast into the sea, turning the water to blood, killing a third of the sea's creatures, and destroying a third of its ships (Rev 8:8–9). The third trumpet brings with it a falling star named Wormwood that turns drinking water into the bitter water of its namesake and poisons many people as a result (Rev 8:10–11). And the fourth brings destruction of one third of the sun, the moon, and the stars, bringing darkness to each (Rev 8:12–13). The fifth trumpet signals a longer vision in which John adapts an ancient myth, describing the fall of evil angels that was later applied to the figure of Satan. In this vignette a single star falls to earth and unleashes locusts that are bent—not on consuming vegetation—but on consuming humankind (Rev 9:1–12). Then in a sixth and lengthier vision the trumpet announces the arrival of three riders whose horses are emissaries of Satan, who unleash plagues that are a call to repentance (Rev 9:13–21).

As in the last set of visions, John introduces an interlude that builds suspense (Rev 10:1–11:13). But the visions described here are not mentioned simply for dramatic effect. By describing the Temple, the bittersweet scroll, and the witnesses, John also brings his hearers back to concerns that might otherwise be lost while listening to his vision.

- The measuring of the Temple reminds the churches of Asia Minor that they are the people of God.
- The recommissioning of John underlines again his God-given authority as prophet, and the invitation to consume the scroll underscores the divine origins of his message.
- The reference to two witnesses summarizes the church's role in the midst of the chaos unleashed by the trumpets.
- The image of the two olive trees that appear by their side alludes to Elijah and Moses who were expected to return on the last day: the church will not be alone in witnessing to its faith.

- The seven peals of thunder that go undescribed signal the imminence of the end; and the churches are reassured of God's sustaining presence.

So here, as elsewhere, John continues to describe a vision, and, at the same time, shape the perceptions of his churches, reinforce his understanding of their identity, and provide them with a justification for the appeal he makes for faithfulness.

Then John turns to the seventh and final trumpet (Rev 11:15–19). The kingdom of the world is declared to be God's. The twenty-four elders reappear, celebrating the occasion in worship, and the divine throne room along with the long-lost ark of the covenant becomes visible. Having returned here and in the interlude to so many of the themes already explored in the book, some hearers may have thought that John's vision was at an end. But the elders hint that there is more to come and announce that it is time to destroy those who destroy the earth (Rev 11:18).

THE WOMAN, THE DRAGON, AND THE CHILD

John introduces a lengthy mythic vignette that describes a cosmic battle for sovereignty (Rev 12:1–14:20). It is probably an independent narrative that originally consisted of more than one story and was neither Jewish nor Christian in origin. But in John's Apocalypse it serves new purposes, bringing his hearers back to the deeper reality behind the events he is describing.

He also continues to deal with time and the future. His vision at this point, however, takes the reader to such a completely different level and so fuses the past, present, and future that time as chronology is all but completely suspended. In so doing the vision serves the same role that the throne room vision did: it lifts the hearer out of their current struggles and, at the same time, offers a picture of what is at stake in the present. Depending upon how one divides the material, here again there may be seven scenes.

> A great portent appeared in heaven: a woman clothed with the sun, with the moon under her feet, and on her head a crown of twelve stars. She was pregnant and was crying out in birth pangs, in the agony of giving birth.
> —REV 12:1–2

In the first scene the three central protagonists are introduced. John witnesses a woman wearing a crown of twelve stars (Rev 12:1–6), representing Israel in terms used to describe Eve in Genesis 3. She is in childbirth and the child—her son—is definitely Jesus. For John, however, what really matters is that the birth of Jesus signals the beginning of the messianic era because that is the era in which his church lives. A dragon with seven heads, ten horns, and seven crowns or diadems on his heads pursues both the woman and the child. At one and the same time, he is Tiamat—the monster from the deep in the Babylonian creation myth; Leviathan, the serpent-monster of Hebrew mythology (Ps 74:14); the serpent from the garden of Eden (Gen 3); and Satan, whom John describes as "deceiver of the whole world" (Rev 12:9). He is all of these things and more because he represents all that is evil and opposed to God. Other characters will join the cast, but these are the principals.

In this first scene, the dragon attempts to destroy the child and the latter is enthroned, hearkening again back to earlier images of the crucified, resurrected, and glorified Christ. Time is immediately relativized, the present redefined. The battle we are witnessing is already over. His mother (the church) escapes to the desert, just as Israel escaped Egyptian pursuit (Rev 12:1–6). To know this is to know something about the future that draws deeply on the past, but is meant to redefine the present. Israel was right to trust God in the wilderness. The church is right to trust God now.

Israel was right to trust God in the wilderness. The church is right to trust God now.

In the second scene, war breaks out in heaven and the archangel Michael leads the opposition to the dragon, who is now identified as Satan. Satan is thrown out of heaven, not to explain his existence, but to underline his defeat in the death and resurrection of Jesus the Lamb (Rev 12:7–12). A voice from heaven announces the victory, notes that it is the blood of not just the Lamb, but the martyred church that has conquered the dragon, and warns that (defeated though he is) the dragon will wreak as much havoc as possible in the time left.

As if to confirm this observation, in the third scene the dragon resumes his pursuit of the mother, using the waters of chaos in an attempt to drown her. When he is unsuccessful, he pursues her children (the church) instead. John describes them as those who keep God's commandments, underlining again the choice between Christ and culture (Rev 12:13–17).

Frustrated by his defeat, in the fourth scene the dragon is joined by an ally—a beast—that emerges from the ocean and shares in the dragon's nature, as its seven heads, seven crowns, and ten horns emphasize. The beast from the sea evokes images of the Empire: the titles on his head reflect the divine titles accorded the emperor; and the wounded beast who returns is an allusion to rumors that Nero was still alive and would return, to persecute the church once again. John's combination of the characteristics of the four animals described in Dan 7 (the lion, the bear, the leopard, and a beast with ten horns) gives his listeners clues to the significance of the beast. This new ruler, like the rulers of Daniel's day, will be judged. The past speaks to the present and defines the future. The faithful—like Daniel, Shadrach, Meshach, and Abednego—are called to endurance (Rev 13:1–10).

Pressing his advantage, in the fifth scene the dragon is joined by a third ally from beneath the earth, completing a demonic trinity that vies with Father, Son, and Holy Spirit for the attention of the world. And the third beast, like the Lamb, marks his followers and competes for their attention as worshipers. His sign is 666—the total achieved by adding up the letters in Nero's name in Hebrew (Rev 13:11–18).

Having described how things "presently *are*," in the last two scenes, John then describes how things will "*finally* be" and, therefore, really are. In scenes one through five, salvation seems to lie in worshiping the emperor. In scene six it is the symbolic 144,000, those who are faithful to the Lamb, that are saved (Rev 14:1–5). In scenes one through five, judgment seems to have been imposed on those who find themselves before Roman civil authorities. In scene seven it is Rome that is judged (Rev 14:6–20).

THE BOWLS OF WRATH

Given the definitive character of this vision, it may seem strange to go back to the pattern of seven seals and trumpets that John used earlier. But in offering a third set of images using the seven bowls of wrath (Rev 15:1–16:21), John is no more interested in chronology here than he has been elsewhere. That is why the bowls of wrath are preceded by a celebration that includes the victors over the dragon and his allies. That is why they stand again in the throne room by the waters of chaos that are now tranquil. And that is why, like true children of Israel, they sing the Song of Moses, which is also the Song of the Lamb:

"Great and amazing are your deeds,
Lord God the Almighty!
Just and true are your ways,
King of the nations!
Lord, who will not fear
and glorify your name?
For you alone are holy.
All nations will come
and worship before you,
for your judgments have been revealed."
(Rev 15:3–4)

The bowls are then emptied. Like the seals and trumpets they have an evocative character that no doubt resonated in more than one way with John's churches. His hearers may have thought of the bronze bowls that were used to carry away hot ash from the altar after sacrifices were burned (Exod 27:3; 38:3; Num 4:14). They may allude to the prayers of the church associated with the golden bowls containing incense already described in Rev 5:8. Or they may refer to the cup of God's wrath described in prophetic literature and elsewhere (Ps 75:8; Isa 51:17; Jer 25:15–29; 49:12).

Then one of the four living creatures gave the seven angels seven golden bowls full of the wrath of God, who lives forever and ever; and the temple was filled with smoke from the glory of God . . . —REV 15:7–8

But carried by angels who emerge from "the Tent of Testimony," which harkens back to Israel's tabernacle in the wilderness (Exod 33:7–11), it is no surprise that each of the seven bowls are modeled on the plagues of Egypt. The "foul and painful sore" (Rev 16:2) echoes Exod 9:8–12. The blood in the sea (Rev 16:3) and the blood poured into rivers and springs (Rev 16:4) both reflect the plague in Exod 7:20–21. The scorching heat of the sun (Rev 16:8) and the darkness poured directly on the throne of the beast (Rev 16:10–11) are free adaptations of the plague described in Exod

10:21–23. The bowl poured out on the Euphrates (Rev 16:12–16) borrows on Exod 8:5–6. And finally, the great hailstorm borrows on the imagery of Exod 9:13–26. The past defines the future and thereby defines the present.

The past defines the future and thereby defines the present.

Two Horizons

How, then, in this section, does John's horizon speak to that of contemporary readers?

- Far from speculating about the future, John is attempting to shape the church's view of his own present.
- Accordingly, while John clearly believes that the church will ultimately be vindicated, his eschatology (his beliefs about the end of time) are not cast in completely futuristic terms.
- For John the reassurance that Christ will vindicate the church is rooted in the conviction that the church's vindication was already won on the cross. Christ may be coming again, but he is already present.
- As a result, time is relativized and the present is redefined. The battle we are witnessing is, in important ways, already over.

In thinking, then, about the implications for our own horizon it is important to realize that speculating about the future based upon John's observations could not be further from what he intended. John is, instead, speaking a word of comfort and encouragement to the present. At times, scholars have argued that the Christian faith is far too deeply invested in a theology of deliverance and cares very little about the moral demands associated with living responsibly in this world; and John's Apocalypse is often blamed for this failure. But it is the roadmap approach, not the Book of Revelation that justifies that criticism. Like the prophets, John describes the future in order to instill spiritual and moral accountability in the present.

A conversation with John's Apocalypse might well begin by asking how our understanding of the future might change the shape of our lives now.

A conversation with John's Apocalypse, then, might well begin by asking how our understanding of the future might change the shape of our lives now. We might also ask, if our eschatology has the same kind of significance for our lives that John believed it should have for his, how would our eschatology change and how would its role in our beliefs be altered?

Continuing the Conversation . . .

On the issue of violence in apocalyptic literature, see Arthur P. Mendel, *Vision and Violence* (Ann Arbor: The University of Michigan Press, 1992); Barbara Rossing, *The Rapture Exposed: The Message of Hope in the Book of Revelation* (Boulder: Westview Press, 2004).

On the culturally conditioned nature of time, see Edward T. Hall, *The Dance of Life: The Other Dimension of Time* (New York: Random House, 1983); Robert H. Lauer, *Temporal Man: The Meaning and Uses of Social Time* (New York: Prager Publishers, 1981).

A Choice of Two Cities: Revelation 17:1–22:21

Live your lives in the City of Babylon or the City of God?

I have a good friend who compares reading the Book of Revelation with catching butterflies:

> I grew up in farm country in central Maryland. We were surrounded by fields and woods, and town (and all 1200 people in it) seemed very far away. When I was 10 or 11 I found a new hobby—I decided to chase butterflies. Not, mind you, just hopping around in mid-air after the butterflies that fluttered over Mother's zinnias and snapdragons, but running through the fields of alfalfa and sweet clover with a net and a jar filled with cotton soaked in formaldehyde. You see, I was serious about this enterprise—I was a junior scientist collecting specimens. I would take the butterflies I captured back to the house and mount them carefully on a padded board and then look in my butterfly book to learn what sort of butterfly I had captured, its range, and its living habits. If I damaged one when I caught it, then I would sometimes dissect it and look at pieces of it under my microscope, or shake some of the butterfly dust from its wings onto a slide to see what that looked like close-up. For a couple of summers I knew quite a lot about butterflies. Monarchs, Viceroys, Yellow Swallowtails and Black Swallowtails . . . The only part of the process that I didn't really enjoy was killing the butter-

flies. But, you see . . . if I was going to learn anything about them, if I was going to really know about butterflies, then I had to kill them and pin them to that board. If, however, the only way you study butterflies is pinned to a board, you will miss quite a lot. You will miss the Swallowtail caterpillars devouring the parsley and dill; the way a Monarch unrolls its proboscis to drink at the edge of a puddle; or the way that wings seem to change color as the sunlight flashes upon them. To learn those sorts of things you must sit still and pay attention with all of your senses while the world of butterflies unfolds around you. It has been a long time since I chased butterflies, and for the last ten years or so there hasn't even been very much time to watch them in my gardens. I have been studying other things. . . . Revelation, however, is a lot like butterflies. You have to know about its structure, how it fits together and about the references it makes to really understand it, but the pieces aren't all there is to it. The real trick here, as with any text from the Bible, is to study it, to learn something about what it means, without killing it and pinning it to a board like a butterfly. Because, when you have finished studying, the word will still be living and you must sit very still, pay attention, and listen as God's word unfolds around you in flashes of color and light.[1]

When dealing with the imagery of John's Apocalypse, this is exactly what the interpreter needs to remember. The stories, actors, and images can be unpacked in some detail; the scriptural allusions are readily identified; and the points of contact with John's churches, the Roman Empire, and the Judaism of his day are all there. Yet, it is equally clear that the "flashes of color and light" cannot be reduced to a one-to-one correspondence.

To put it another way, John's use of imagery is like the brush-strokes in an impressionist's painting. You can only grasp the artist's intention when the painting is seen as a whole. Stand too close, squint at the individual brushstrokes, and the image is diminished or disappears completely. It is that larger picture that John meant for his hearers to *see* with their ears.

A Choice between Cities

This is as clear in Rev 17–22 as it is anywhere in the Apocalypse. The mythic looms large again, but there can be no doubt that we are talking about the human city of Rome and the church in Asia Minor, living in faithfulness to its Lord.

John's decision to use cities (Babylon and Jerusalem) as the central metaphor for the choice facing his church is a natural one. The Apostle Paul, his famous predecessor, had consciously chosen to begin spreading the gospel in cities, and, as a result, they figured prominently in the well-being of the ancient church. The world in which John lived was also city-centered. For 650 years rulers used them to spread their vision and build a power base. Alexander, Augustus, and others throughout the period also used cities to stabilize the regions in which their cities were located. It was there that they garrisoned their troops, established courts, and developed the bureaucratic procedures needed to maintain roads and collect taxes. So, it is no surprise to find that cities acquired an emblematic significance or that John would cast the choice facing his readers as one between the city of Babylon and the Holy City. But John's use of the image, like butterflies and impressionist paintings, is not exhausted by historical and social explanations for their existence.

> *John's use of imagery is like the brushstrokes in an impressionist's painting.*

He is, instead, intentionally tapping his church's memory and emotions, conjuring up two cities that loom large in the imagination. In this last section of his Apocalypse, he turns his attention to each city, announcing that one will be judged (Rev 17–18) and that the other will triumph (Rev 19–22). In so doing, he puts the choice between Christ and culture before his readers a final time, confronting some and comforting others.

> *. . . and on her forehead was written a name, a mystery: "Babylon the great, mother of whores and of earth's abominations." —REV 17:5*

THE JUDGMENT OF BABYLON, AKA ROME

The first of those cities is Babylon. Known to ancient Jews as the center of Mesopotamian society, it is—in one sense—simply another ancient and now by-gone city. But as the capital of the empire that captured Jerusalem in 597 BCE, it looms far larger in memory and myth. It is the city of exile, a place of bondage, and the enemy of God.

John knows this and taps into the visceral, even repulsive set of associations that this ancient city has with his congregations. He paints a lurid picture that builds on these associations, characterizing Babylon as a whore who is sexually promiscuous and actively seduces all those around her (Rev 17:1f.). Lest his hearers conclude that her conduct has little or no bearing on their lives, he goes on to note that she is "drunk with the blood of the saints and the blood of the witnesses to Jesus" (Rev 17:6).

Then capitalizing on the surprise that ancient Babylon could be the undoing of the church, John makes it clear that this archetypal city is, in fact, Rome (Rev 17:6bf.), the city set between seven hills and governed by seven emperors (Rev 17:9), the last of whom will be a beast—Nero revisited (Rev 17:11). With this observation it becomes clear, in retrospect, that the whore John has been describing is the city whose patroness and goddess Roma is worshipped in Asia Minor (Rev 2:1, 8, 12). According to the world over which she rules, she is the source of blessing. Even in the eyes of her enemies and victims she is large, dominant, and defining. In spite of the pain that she inflicts, it is difficult to imagine a world without her; and the water on which she rides—the other nations of the world—are, for that reason, her allies (Rev 17:2, 15).

But in the war that she is about to wage with her allies against the Lamb, she will be defeated and the victory will belong to the Son and to those that follow him (Rev 17:14). When the outcome is clear, then even her allies will turn against her (Rev 17:16–18) and the self-destructive nature of evil will be manifest.

In what one commentator rightly describes as one of Scripture's more poignant passages, John then both celebrates and mourns the undoing of Rome (Rev 18). The ambivalence of this lament that combines elements of dirge and taunt may reflect the ambivalence of John's own followers. Some of John's congregations no doubt celebrated the promised demise of the Empire. But not everyone who agreed with him probably viewed the passing of Rome as a completely positive development and those who disagreed with John, no doubt, objected (cf. Rev 18:2, 21–23).

So, here again, the complex shape of his churches and the pastoral demands John faces are in evidence. The lament acknowledges the pain that some experience at the prospect of Rome's demise; or he may be skewering the self-interest that those who depend upon Rome can display. John may have even been attempting to address specific misgivings, organized as the laments are around the grief of kings, merchants, and sailors; or they may simply reflect the groups who most often depended upon the Empire. But whether that is the case or not, John no doubt knew that those feelings would surface. And whether or not he shared their ambivalence, he undoubtedly knew that without acknowledging it and challenging it some might not hear.

He also clearly felt that the judgment levied against Rome was justified. So the lament outlines the case against the city:

- idolatrous worship (Rev 18:3)
- violence against the church and others (Rev 18:24)
- "blasphemous self-glorification" (Rev 18:3, 7, 9)
- the wanton use of its wealth (Rev 18:3, 11–19, 23)

Anticipating that indictment, the angel who announces the fall of Babylon, aka Rome (Rev 18:2), also cries out to the church, "Come out of her, my people, so that you do not take part in her sins, and so that you do not share in her plagues; for her sins are heaped high as heaven, and God has remembered her iniquities" (Rev 18:4–5).

THE REDEMPTION OF THE HOLY CITY, AKA THE CITY OF GOD

Then in chapters 19–22, John announces the coming of the Holy City. Each of the major divisions in the Book of Revelation begin with a glimpse into the transcendent, deeper realities that John believes should shape the behavior of his church, and each is followed by visions offered in sets of seven. Here, in the last of the visions, John takes his readers back to the divine throne room and following hard on the words of praise and worship uttered around the heavenly throne by the twenty-four elders (Rev 19:1–11) are the last seven visions:

- the *Parousia* or return of Christ (Rev 19:11–16)
- the last battle (Rev 19:17–21)
- the binding of Satan (Rev 20:1–3)
- the millennium (Rev 20:4–6)
- the defeat of Gog and Magog (Rev 20:7–10)
- the last judgment (Rev 20:11–15)
- and the New Jerusalem (Rev 19:11–22:21)

Here, as elsewhere, it is a mistake to assume that John has a chronological interest in the events described. Some of them might have been given in a different order. Some of them overlap or happen all but simultaneously and he abandons numbering completely.

It is also a mistake to reduce the "flashes of color and light" to a one-to-one correspondence with past, present, and future events, or to focus on the brushstrokes to the exclusion of the image that John is painting. Unlike the defeat of Rome and other emblematic cities of power, the final triumph of the Holy City is without precedent and without point of contact in history. So, while John has used images of an evocative kind throughout the Apocalypse, here those used are, by definition, among the ones more thoroughly rooted in myth and imagination.

Parousia

It is not surprising, for that reason, to discover that when John begins offering picture after picture of that triumph, he focuses first not on the coming of *something*, but of *someone* (Rev 19:11–16). The coming of the Lamb—the resurrected and glorified Christ—is, by definition, central to John's expectation. Not because of its place in a set of chronologically ordered events, but because the Lamb is the church's redeemer and champion. Whatever else one might imagine about the coming of the Holy City, it is all but impossible to imagine it without the Lamb.

> Then I saw heaven opened, and there was a white horse! Its rider is called Faithful and True, and in righteousness he judges and makes war.
> —REV 19:11

The details that contribute to this first picture cannot be exhausted in describing what John intends, but citing a few of them hints at the larger impression he is trying to convey.

- Jesus arrives on a white horse (Rev 19:11), supplanting the first of the four riders in Rev 6:2. The color of his mount suggests both victory and purity.
- His title "Faithful and True" (Rev 19:11) underwrites the authority and reliability he is accorded in the message of the seven letters to the seven churches in Rev 3:14.
- He is described as the Word of God, emphasizing his divine nature. As "King of Kings and Lord of Lords," he rightly bears

the titles that Nero and others have attempted to appropriate for themselves (Rev 19:16).

▪ And, perhaps most significantly, he wears a robe soaked in his own blood, alluding to his sacrifice on the cross and the death of his followers (Rev 19:13).[2]

In this regard, John's description of the coming of Christ stands in stark contrast with a good deal of left-behind theology. Contemporary interpreters are often engrossed with endless details associated with the demise of the wicked. While John's vision is not without its lurid details, the first thing that he does is to take his readers back to the earliest images offered in the Apocalypse, underlining again the authority of the resurrected Christ. Roadmap-readings often stress the judgment imposed on the wicked, and that theme no doubt appears in the Apocalypse. But the army that accompanies the Lamb into battle is not dressed for it. Wearing white festival robes, John takes his hearers back again visually to the obligations he outlined at the beginning in the seven letters to the seven churches.

Last Battle

Some of the same differences apply to John's description of the last battle that is certainly marked by shocking violence (Rev 19:11–16). That violence raises serious moral and theological problems. But it is worth noting that the battle John describes has one combatant—the Lamb. His followers, who are symbolically present, are not called upon to lift a sword. They are not invited to decide who should be judged. And they are not offered enticements to engage in the conflict. In a sense, they stand alongside the Lamb only by virtue of having responded faithfully to the resurrected Christ's appeal for obedience.

That, no doubt, is why the one and only weapon used by the Lamb is the word (Rev 19:21). The conflict that follows is a battle with two sides locked in combat, but the sides are chosen, not on the basis of racial or national identity, or by socioeconomic standing. Instead, the free and the enslaved, the small and the great, are aligned with the beast by virtue of their response to the word. As such the battle that John describes is an unflinching recognition that the forces of sin and evil cannot be simply excused or overlooked.

Told in this way, the description of the last battle also mitigates against an easy identification with a group or an ideology. Having named the differences in his own church with the seven letters, John's vision challenges his hearers to consider whether they are (as one interpreter puts it) the dinner guests or the menu.[3] While some roadmap-readings of the Apocalypse have seemingly suggested that one can read the description of judgment that John gives with an eye to guessing who will be punished, John seems far more intent on getting his hearers to weigh carefully which side of the last battle each of them has chosen to take.

The Binding of Satan

The same challenge is implicit in the binding of Satan, which (like the other visions of the Holy City) John offers as yet another impressionistic painting of what lies ahead. Here his pastoral concerns are again in evidence. The human manifestations of evil—the beast and the false prophet—have already been vanquished, but there is the larger question of Satan who is evil reified and whose influence continues to be felt. One can almost hear, the "Yes, but . . ." in the response of John's churches to their promised deliverance. The objection that evil still holds sway accounts not only for this vignette, but for John's concession that the days to come may not immediately hold complete deliverance from Satan's influence. Hence the binding of Satan isn't meant to be taken literally.

Nonetheless, drawing on ancient Jewish images (Isa 24:22; 1 Enoch 10:4–10), John describes evil as a force in the world that will be neutralized. "Seized," "bound," "thrown," "locked," and "sealed," this is no force of power on a par with that of God. Satan's defeat is assured. God is in control.

Here, then, as elsewhere the description John offers is not designed to indulge speculation about the nature or fate of Satan. He is the serpent and deceiver. But the angel dispatched from heaven has also bound him and, for that reason, he now lacks control over anyone. In that sense, the description speaks to the fears of those who are overwhelmed and the confusion of those who have been deceived. Neither fate is inevitable. John's hearers need to choose, and they can choose now knowing the deeper truth about the evil that seemingly holds sway.

The Millennium

Nowhere is the influence of roadmap-readings more in evidence than in the place attributed to the millennium. A seminal distinction, the approach such interpreters take is one that divides them into pre-, post-, and a-millennial camps. But from a historical-critical point of view, what we are dealing with here in John's fourth painting of the future is a brief vignette so short, and positioned so unobtrusively, that it hardly justifies so much attention.

What John has in mind here justifies attention, but it is not the linchpin in a complex chronology of final or eschatological events. Instead, borrowing on established expectations in Jewish tradition that can be found in both prophetic (Isa 65:20f.) and apocalyptic literature (Dan 7:9), John is speaking pastorally to those who know the martyred. They may rest assured that those who have died will be resurrected and they will reign with Christ as priests and kings.

> What we are dealing with here in John's fourth painting of the future is a brief vignette so short, and positioned so unobtrusively, that it hardly justifies so much attention.

In picturing the martyrs as reigning on earth, it is also clear that John was still inclined to affirm the goodness of God's creation as well. So, like Paul, one might imagine that John, too, felt that the world around him was in birth pangs that presaged a complete transformation of God's creation. In that respect, too, John's vision is very different from the tenor of some roadmap-readings and even some secular apocalyptic ones that visualize a church jettisoned or "raptured" from a dying planet.

The Defeat of Gog and Magog

Throughout the composition of his Apocalypse, John drew extensively on the visions of Ezekiel and here, perhaps more than anywhere else in his book, it is clear that John felt bound to repeat details from Ezekiel that he may or may not have otherwise included. Gog *of* Magog or Gog *Prince of* Magog appears in Ezek 38–39. Beyond his role as leader of the forces of evil against the people of God, little or nothing is known about him. In Ezekiel all that is clear is that Gog is from a place called Magog. It was only over time that the understanding of the phrase was garbled and came to be thought of not as one person, but two and not as one nation, but two.

The release of Satan, who fights alongside both countries, is dictated by John's theology that Satan is not simply the deceiver of individuals, but of nations as well. So there is something of a dramatic judgment made here by John that allows for Satan's release from bondage (Rev 20:7). But the effort to find two countries in John's day (never mind two countries in our own!) is a misguided effort and misses the point (Rev 20:8).

That said, John may have more in mind than simply a slavish conformity to the outline of Ezekiel's vision. As one scholar points out, the primary reason for including this particular painting in his gallery may, in fact, revolve around the conduct of Satan, the nations, and the saints—each of which provides a different cautionary tale. In the case of Satan, for example, his insistence on fomenting rebellion, even in the face of repeated defeat (Rev 19:9–20:3), may have served as a reminder to the church that the call to faithfulness could not be ignored. Apparent well-being would not prevent Satan from resuming his efforts whenever he chose. Similarly, the capacity of the nations to be deceived—yet again!—may have been meant to suggest that the church could not assume that the structural evil they had encountered in the Empire was likely to disappear from the face of an unredeemed world. If that was the case, then that may well explain why, when Gog and Magog attack, the saints of God are encamped in something that looks like ancient Israel's sojourning wilderness nation. There is no security apart from God.

> Then I saw a great white throne and the one who sat on it; the earth and the heaven fled from his presence, and no place was found for them. —REV 20:11

The Last Judgment

In this judgment scene, the discreet "flashes of color and light" used in each scene are again in evidence. The martyrs have been resurrected and the righteous enthroned as priests and kings, but here again is everyone who has ever died—"great and small"—before the throne of God (Rev 20:12). The two books that are for the proceedings echo the tension between faith and works that is forever at the heart of the Christian faith. One records the actions of those who stand before the throne, underlining the utter seriousness of the choices John's readers make. The other book—the book of life—is governed alone by God's gracious choice.

Again, the moral significance of the vision is clear. And speculation about where and how this all happens as part of a timetable is a completely misplaced concern. In attempting to move his congregations to a single place in their understanding of the crisis they face, John is anxious to balance the importance of the people's dependence upon God with their own responsibility for their actions. So, while there is deliverance to be had and death itself will be destroyed (Rev 20:14), John also leaves his hearers in no doubt that those who fail to respond will be "thrown into the lake of fire" (Rev 20:15).

The New Jerusalem

John abandons all the smaller canvases and begins to paint a final mural. The place of this vision at the end of his Apocalypse and the expansive visual character of it all explains why these verses (21:1–22:21) have figured so prominently in the worship of the church; and they are the best possible argument against left-behind theology that is preoccupied with, well, being left behind! Here juxtaposed at last with John's picture of Babylon is his imaginative portrait of the New Jerusalem, aka the City of God. And the larger choice that he has pressed throughout the Apocalypse is now set out in dramatic relief.

John's followers may not have visited Rome, but they have never lived a day without being made aware of its significance for their lives. The troops garrisoned in their cities, the worship of the emperor, the vast network of roads spreading across the Mediterranean, the ships anchored in their harbors, and the courts before which they have been tried are all manifestations of Rome's influence. Under the spell of such an influence it is perilously easy to imagine that there are no choices to be made.

But, here in the closing lines of his Apocalypse, John paints a picture of the alternative. Drawing extensively on the Jewish tradition, he recasts images that are widely used in the Hebrew Bible, including the descriptions of the streets and gates (Isa 60:11–14), the jewels

And I saw the holy city, the new Jerusalem, coming down out of heaven from God, prepared as a bride adorned for her husband.
—REV 21:2

used in the walls and foundation (Exod 28:17–21; 39:10–14), and the presence of the tree of life (1 Enoch 25:5). Image upon image is used to describe the aspirations of God's people and, freely combined, the features of the city amount to an ideal that is far larger than any decoding of the images could possibly yield.

The dangers of pinning the butterfly to a board, or of scrutinizing the brushstrokes to the exclusion of the painting, are inescapable. Particularly when one realizes that, for all the detail he offers, the city of God is, for John, nothing more and nothing less than the presence of God. As the city descends, a voice declares,

> See, the home of God is among mortals.
> He will dwell with them;
> they will be his peoples,
> and God himself will be with them.
> (Rev 21:3)

It is God who comforts the people and who wipes away their tears. In his presence death no longer exists (Rev 21:4). The inhabitants of the city see God face to face and they bear his name on their foreheads (Rev 22:4). They are surrounded by his glory, as is reflected in the jasper walls of the city (Rev 21:11) and even the dimensions of the city itself are designed to suggest that God is "directly, intimately available" (Rev 21:15-16).[4]

Even here, however, John doesn't lose sight of the crisis facing his churches with which the letters began. The city to which they are invited is also a holy city without "the cowardly, the faithless, the polluted, the murderers, the fornicators, the sorcerers, the idolaters, and all liars" (Rev 21:8). So, while John describes a vision of a city entered by grace and marked by intimacy with God, it is also clear that the inhabitants have grasped the demands of the gospel. The description could not have been lost on John's congregations. One cannot help but wonder if John would have warmed to the definition of heaven and hell that C. S. Lewis once offered, arguing that the essence of heaven is the presence of God and the essence of hell,

God's absence. What we receive in the next life is, he argued, what we most wanted in this one.[5]

Vision and Reality

The alphabetic mind—the mind oriented to print—knows when a book has reached its end. The pages run out, the back cover grows closer and closer, the final margin may reveal a blank space. The oral mind requires some indication that the end is approaching as well, and it needs to be announced.

John knows this intuitively. Knowing, too, that he has taken his congregations beyond their daily experience into the deeper nature of reality, time, and the future, he may have also sensed that the need was particularly acute in this case.

It was not, however, a matter of bringing his audience back to reality. The deeper reality of place, time, and the future is what he has been describing to them. What was needed was a means of bringing his audience back into the moment, transformed by a vision of the realities he had revealed to them.

And, so, he announces the end of the vision, reaffirming its revelatory character (Rev 22:8). He stresses the imminence of the end and, therefore, the urgency of the situation (Rev 22:10); and he calls his congregations to a faithful response (Rev 22:11). The Lamb then speaks the closing words to the church.

A benediction of grace rests upon those who respond and wash their robes in the blood of the Lamb (Rev 22:14). If an increasing number of scholars are right, following these words of reassurance, those who heard John's Apocalypse may have received Eucharist. As they did they would have been reminded of his victory and the reassurance of his promise: "Surely I am coming soon" (Rev 22:20).

Two Horizons

The use of imagery in John's Apocalypse makes a literal reading of the book inappropriate. It also underlines the danger of treating the imagery as something to be decoded. Indeed, such literalizing of John's images—far from affirming the reality behind those images—trivializes it.

Describing the political and social realities of his day, John's imagery has points of contact with real people, places, and events. But it is also evocative in character, tapping deep wells of hope and imagination. He also describes experiences without precedent in history that are even more plainly evocative in character.

That John sometimes taps into a sense of revulsion and even prejudice in giving expression to his views cannot and should not be ignored. Not all of what we learn from Scripture is to be emulated. As in the so-called imprecatory Psalms that call for God to punish the writers' enemies, what we learn at times is that fear, social pressure, marginalization, and persecution can breed self-righteousness, anger, and a thirst for revenge.

Here as elsewhere in John's Apocalypse, John's message to the churches of Asia Minor underlines the urgency of a question that we all need to answer.

Here as elsewhere in John's Apocalypse, however, his message to the churches of Asia Minor underlines the urgency of a question that we all need to answer. Anyone who subscribes to the conviction that a person of faith must engage the world will face a choice between the cities of our own making and God's. There will always be questions of where and how those choices manifest themselves and should be made. How much John or the members of his church accurately understood those issues in their own day is open to debate. But the question is inescapable.

Final Thoughts: Listening to a Vision

I am not a devotee of what people in the United States call late night television. But I am just old enough to know that one of the earliest hosts of such programs was a man by the name of Johnny Carson. Before David Letterman's "Top Ten" lists and Jay Leno's "Headlines," Carson experimented with a routine he called "Carnac the Magnificent."

In that routine he wrapped his head in a towel, imitating an ancient fortune-teller. Holding cards to his forehead with "answers" written on them, Carnac was supposedly able to divine the corresponding questions. Most of the answers and the questions are so thoroughly rooted in time and place as to be of little or no relevance any longer. Even the jokes imbedded in the questions he asked required a fairly good knowledge of US pop-culture of the day.

But Carnac's effort is a fitting image for what I would like to do in the final pages of this book, because essentially I would like to spend just a bit of time answering questions I think that you might want to ask. Just how perceptive I have been, only you will be able to say.

1. *Did John really see a vision?*

The answer? I suppose it is possible. A friend of mine observes that God speaks to us by whatever means we expect; and if John expected a vision—on that reading of it—God may have spoken to John in a vision. But I have no idea how to prove or disprove that assumption.

If you are asking me, what do *I* think, I would say no. John has made such complex use of scriptural and historical allusions that I find it hard to believe that a visionary experience of some kind was at the heart of John's composition. It is far more likely that apocalyptic literature served as a literary vehicle, designed to lend authority and interest to his reflections.

But, then, I see no downside to that conclusion. The place that Scripture occupies in the life of the church as sacred literature should not obscure its human character. Letters, words, sentences, differing genres of literature, and very real historical circumstances are the arena in which our understanding of God is hammered out.

2. *Did John expect God to intervene soon and, if so, was he mistaken?*

Yes and yes. I do not believe that the language of John's Apocalypse can be pushed for exacting concrete details. But I do believe that he expected God to intervene immediately, publicly, and dramatically. And God did not.

In this respect he was not alone. More than one person in the first century of the church's experience expected God to intervene soon on behalf of the church. There are echoes of that expectation in Mark's Gospel (chapter 13) and in 1 Thessalonians (4:13f.).

But the fact that God did not intervene in John's day is a problem for us, not for John. For John, as with so many of his predecessors—both Jewish and Christian—such expectations were ultimately predicated upon a confidence in God's goodness, not in the reliability of a timetable. That is why so many of the expectations were recycled and appeared over and over again in apocalyptic literature. They trusted in God, no matter what transpired. We trust in God, if we find that our expectations have been fulfilled.

3. What do I make of the violent, one might say occasionally vengeful, character of John's Apocalypse?

It will depend in large part upon the attitude that you take toward Scripture. If you believe that the inspiration of Scripture requires you to read it from start to finish in a prescriptive fashion, then you will be forced by the logic of your position to do just that. But I am inclined to believe that Scripture, although it is inspired by an encounter with God, cannot be flatly or woodenly read.

Some of what John felt and hoped for was no doubt shaped by the anger, anxiety, and frustration that he felt as he navigated the crisis facing his church. So, as with the imprecatory psalms that call on God to punish the writer's enemies, we are drawn into a conversation with God about the anger, anxiety, and frustration that, from time to time, we all feel. To find it in John's Apocalypse and elsewhere in Scripture should give us permission to admit that we have those feelings as well; and it should underline the spiritual challenge we face in grappling with our own capacity for cruelty. But it should not be read as authorization to inflict the same kind of pain on others or to pray for God to inflict it.

4. Wouldn't we be better off simply doing away with eschatology?

That's a tough one. Ask me on a day when I am confronted with left-behind theology on a regular basis and I am tempted to say yes. In fact, if the choice were one between bad eschatology and no eschatology at all, on balance I would be glad to do without it. Left-behind theology has severed the nerve of moral obligation, leaving some Christians with the impression that it is enough to "hunker down" and wait for the end, instead of engaging the world around them. It has nurtured a zero-sum spirituality that all but shouts, "I can't go to heaven, unless you go to hell." And it has trivialized eschatological expectation that casts God in the role of cosmic partisan.

John's message and the message of Christian eschatology is that we need not stay engaged without hope.

But, in fact, to do away with eschatology of the right kind would completely change the character of the Christian message and make it all but completely impossible to talk about hope or justice. Christians are called to engage the world around us and to work for justice and peace in the name of Christ. But no one who listens to the news can imagine for a moment that any of those efforts are ever entirely successful.

> Then the angel showed me the river of the water of life, bright as crystal, flowing from the throne of God and of the Lamb through the middle of the street of the city. —REV 22:1–2

Without suggesting for a moment that we should "hunker down" and wait for the end, John's message and the message of Christian eschatology is that we need not stay engaged without hope. Nor, like John, do we even need to imagine *the one thing* that—when it comes—will make it all right, because what we wait for is *someone*.

Continuing the Conversation . . .

On the nature of apocalyptic imagery and its use, see Adela Yarbro Collins, *Crisis and Catharsis: The Power of the Apocalypse* (Philadelphia: The Westminster Press, 1984); Stephen D. O'Leary, *Arguing the Apocalypse: A Theory of Millennial Rhetoric* (New York: Oxford, 1994).

On the theology of John's Apocalypse, see Richard Bauckham, *The Theology of the Book of Revelation: New Testament Theology* (ed. James D. G. Dunn; Cambridge: Cambridge University Press, 1993).

On the significance of urban centers in ancient Chritianity, see Wayne A. Meeks, *The First Urban Christians: The Social World of the Apostle Paul* (New Haven, Conn.: Yale University Press, 1983).

ACKNOWLEDGMENTS

No one writes an introduction of this kind without being indebted to people known and unknown, remembered and forgotten. What we both learn and share with others about the biblical text is something we can never claim as our own. So, whatever I say here by way of acknowledgment will touch on only a fraction of the debts I owe.

One such debt is owed to those who read earlier drafts of this manuscript. Thanks go to Dr. Jaime Clark-Soles, friend, colleague, inveterate racquetball opponent, and assistant professor of New Testament Studies at Perkins School of Theology, who gave me the benefit of her expertise. So, too, Ms. Teri Walker, who took great care to read the manuscript with an eye to the needs of those who are likely to read this book.

I also owe a special debt of gratitude to the Reverend Dr. David Schlafer, the people at Church of the Redeemer in Bethesda, Maryland, and their rector, the Reverend Susan Burns. Together, they provided me with important feedback on both the content of this manuscript and on the early page design for the Conversations with Scripture series.

Here, as in all the work that I have done with Morehouse Publishing, I am also grateful to Debra Farrington, my editor and the publisher for this series. Debra has consistently brought her considerable gifts as a writer and editor to bear on all that I have written. The result has always been a book that is stronger than the first effort.

I also owe a word of thanks to others at Morehouse, including Ryan Masteller who was involved in the cover design; Jeff Hamilton, who has helped bring the series to the attention of an ever-wider audience; and Frank Buhrman who provided information for reviewers and the press. Beth Oberholtzer, who has assisted the folks at Morehouse, deserves credit for the elegant and creative approach to page design for this and the other volumes in the series; and the Reverend Helen McPeak created the reflective space needed to weigh the significance of John's Apocalypse for our own lives by crafting the thought-provoking questions that are found here.

Nothing that I ever do is accomplished without the love, support, and counsel of my wife, Elaine, and my daughter, Lindsay. I could endlessly dedicate every word that I write to them, confident that they are, either directly or indirectly, the inspiration of anything good to be found in it.

STUDY QUESTIONS

the Reverend Helen McPeak

Valuing scholarship and accessibility, the Reverend Dr. Frederick W. Schmidt brings his expertise to bear upon the task of reclaiming and "unpacking" Scripture. With academic insight grounded in an awareness of the layperson's day-to-day life, Schmidt invites us into a healthy and helpful relationship with John's vision. This study illuminates a vital piece of apocalyptic literature for the person of thinking faith as it educates the reader about various approaches to Revelation and important contextual and interpretive details of the text. These questions are meant to aid the reader's consideration of Revelation, taking different angles to assist in a broad connection with John's book. A good resource for parish study, this section can be used partially or as a whole.

Introduction

Before you begin, jot down a few sentences about each of the following:

- Why you are engaging in this study of Revelation.
- What you remember hearing earlier in your life about Revelation.
- What you expect of this study.

Pray together the prayer offered at the start of the book.

- In what kinds of situations in your life do you seek faith, courage, strength, and/or hope?
- Why might these be needed now?
- How is it for you to pray this prayer?

Schmidt introduces this study series by commenting on the enormous variety encompassed by Anglicanism, including approach to Scripture.

- Review the four descriptors he offers (pp. xi–xiv).
- Which of these resonates well with you? Why?
- Where is your discomfort?

Schmidt comments, "We know the Bible was shaped by the language, culture, and issues of worlds that no longer exist as such" (p. xv).

- What are the implications of this reality for our approach to the Bible?
- How does this reality interplay with the reality that many of us have "also lived in [the Bible] . . . inhabited it, through worship, preaching, teaching and meditation" (p. xi)?

Schmidt states that people today read the book of Revelation with a Bible-as-roadmap-to-the-future view, if they read it at all (p. xvii).

- What has been your approach to this writing, if any?
- How did you come to this?

Review Schmidt's four-point outline of what you will find in this study (see p. xviii). Hold these points in your consciousness as you continue your reading.

- Do you share his hopes for the results of this study?

Schmidt will address the text of John's Revelation in particular sections later in the book. For now, read the piece as a whole.

- What themes and images stand out for you?
- What questions come into focus as you experience John's vision?
- How do you feel about this writing?

Chapter One: Revelation as Roadmap

According to Schmidt, a "roadmap-reading" approach to interpreting Revelation "enjoys the presumption of being the right way to read this difficult book" (p. 1). It offers the reader "a rough idea of what will happen next."

- How might this be positive? How negative?
- Where do you long to know what lies ahead?

Many specific and possibly unfamiliar terms are used in Schmidt's presentation of the history of the roadmap-reading approach. Choose several of these terms and look them up in a dictionary (standard, theological, of the Christian Church):

- millennialist (pre-, post-, a-millennialist), chiliast, dispensationalist
- pre-, post-, mid-tribulationalist, historicist, futurist
- Montanus, Tertullian, Justin Martyr, Papias, Irenaus

(You may as well go ahead and look up "recrudescence," too.)

What would be necessary for (some of) these words to become part of your daily vocabulary?

Catalog the assumptions Schmidt lists as being made by most, if not all, of the interpretations that take this roadmap approach, including the "deeper assumptions" on page 5.

- Which of these assumptions do you accept? Which do you reject?
- Is it because they make logical sense to you? Is it a gut-level feeling?
- What evidence supports or denies the assumptions?

Schmidt cites Tim LaHaye's noteworthy observation, most people "'don't take the Bible literally. They categorize and mythologize it and read into it their own preconceived ideas. They don't think a loving God will send people to hell.' He will" (p. 6).

- How do you respond to LaHaye's observation?
- What do you suppose was his intention in making it?

Revisit Schmidt's basic elements of left-behind salvation on page 12.

- Where do these elements invite us to focus (e.g., individual, family, community, nation, global population)?
- Do these elements invite action? In what ways?

Are you "getting" this?

- What do you need to better absorb "this extraordinary part of the Greek Testament" (p. 2)?

Chapter Two: Revelation as Myth

Schmidt offers the definition of myth as "not just a fairy tale, but . . . also a bit of narrative or an image used to describe in an evocative fashion the real and deeper nature of an experience, event, or person" (p. 17). Myths function "not only [to] pluck at our heartstrings, but also [to] shape our thinking and prompt us to act."

- Look up "myth" in an etymological dictionary.
- What roles has mythology played in your own edification?
- Name some myths of your own culture, explicit or implicit.

Do some further research on the theologians Schmidt refers to in his discussion of Revelation as myth: Origen, Dionysius, Eusebius, Augustine of Hippo, Joachim of Fiore, Jacques Ellul, and Catherine Keller. (A theological dictionary can offer a brief exposition. Also check out the youth nonfiction section of your library for some easily approachable texts.)

- If you had to vote one of these "most popular" at the moment, whom would you choose? Why?

According to Schmidt, the net result of Origen's approach was "a religious and cultural amalgam that placed a premium upon the spiritual over the material (p. 19).

- Is a premium placed upon the spiritual over the material in our culture?
- What priorities exist here and now?
- How might these priorities influence your study?

Dionysius is cited as taking the view that "the interpretation of the various sections is largely a mystery, something too wonderful for our comprehension . . . but I suspect that some *deeper meaning* is concealed in the words" (p. 20).

- What is your expectation of your own relationship with this writing?

Schmidt includes several amusingly strong verbal attacks in his discussion, e.g., "For he seems to have been a man of very small intelligence, to judge from his books" (Eusebius on p. 20).

- How is it for you to see this side of the Church Fathers' interaction?

Schmidt offers significant discussion of Augustine's reasons for supporting the inclusion of Revelation in the fledgling church's Scriptures.

- What sacred literature is read as part of worship in your community?
- Who decides what will be read? What criteria are used?

Schmidt asserts that for Augustine, sacred literature was the story of "God's effort to redeem humankind working in and through history . . . and should be read as such" (p. 22). Augustine divided sacred history into six parts (see p. 22).

- What reason do you see for his divisions?
- What role does Revelation play in telling the story?

Review Schmidt's list of convictions that shaped the mythic approach to Scripture (p. 23).

- How do you relate to these convictions? What would you change?

Native American storytellers often say things like, "I don't know if this is how it really happened, but I know that it is true." In discussing the fact that those who favored the roadmap approach tended to equate myth with falsehood, Schmidt states, "If what John described wasn't real, then it wasn't true and that conclusion was hardly acceptable" (p. 24).

- In what ways are these opposing views attractive to you?
- Where do you prefer the historians' commitment to finding meaning of the text in its historical setting?

Schmidt cites Ellul as suggesting "that the absence of a relationship with God insured that they could not understand Scripture properly, in spite of all their learning" (p. 25).

- How does your relationship with God or lack thereof influence your participation in this study?

Schmidt points to looking for "the patterns that reappear time and time again throughout history that are either reflective of God's presence or in opposition to it" (p. 29) as one of the strengths of the mythic reading of Revelation. An example is Ellul's structuring of the writing into five sections with seven elements each:

- the church as it is now
- the meaning of history
- Jesus as Lord of both the church and history
- history's end
- the church as it shall be

- How is this kind of pattern helpful to your reading of John's vision?
- How does it distract from finding a deeper meaning?

Chapter Three: Revelation as History

In this chapter, Schmidt introduces the historical-critical approach to biblical criticism, describing "the historical setting of a text as an important key to its meaning" (p. 31).
- What has been your experience with this approach?
- When does Schmidt say historical criticism began? How have conceptions of history changed over time?
- How do you respond to Schmidt's statement that "Certain circumstances usually require us to write and we write in hopes of shaping the circumstances" (p. 33)?

Review the list of clues to Revelation's specific context that loom large from the Bible, according to Schmidt. Schmidt writes that all "scholars can know about *who* wrote the book was that his name was John and he considered himself a prophet" (p. 33).
- How is this information helpful to your understanding of the Book of Revelation?

Schmidt concludes "a somewhat stronger argument is to be made for those who date the Apocalypse to the reign of Domitian" (p. 37). Find other presentations of church and world history of this time to supplement your understanding of the period. (Again, the public library may have useful resources in creating a general overview.)
- What challenges, themes, or patterns present themselves throughout history?
- What is unique to this period?

Schmidt states that "the Apocalypse is both a call for faithfulness under circumstances that [John] feared would erode the commitment of the community and an effort to shape the perceptions of that community in a fashion that would prompt it to take that call seriously" (p. 39).

- Review the factors that contributed to "the sense of tension, crisis, and alienation that John and some of his circle felt." (See pp. 37–39.)
- In what ways are these factors foreign to your life?
- In what ways can you sympathize with John's audience?

Schmidt reminds us that "there is no necessary connection between the practice of criticism and a loss of faith, let alone hostility to it." He continues, "Ultimately, the critical process of raising and answering questions should involve probing not only the words and worlds of the biblical text, but the information and perspectives that help us to understand those worlds more completely" (p. 40).

- Where in your life has "the critical process of raising and answering questions" been a positive experience?
- How have you been trained to tune your inner ear to God's voice "speak[ing] to us *in and through life* . . . always at work in the world" (pp. 40–41)?

Schmidt relates his experiences of using *The Wizard of Oz* as an example of historical criticism in his undergraduate course. (See pp. 41–44.)

- What was your own reaction to the information presented?
- What is to be learned from recent research's deflating these theories?
- How is it for you to allow the interpretation of scriptural texts to be similarly vulnerable?

Schmidt concludes his "opening gambit in support of a historical-critical approach to the interpretation of John's Apocalypse" (p. 42) by writing, "without some idea of the author's intended meaning, there is, in the final analysis, no means of knowing what a passage does or does not mean or of adjudicating between interpretations" (p. 43).

- How are you equipped to approach these texts?
- Who will accompany you in discovering this vital information in reading Revelation as well as the rest of Scripture?

■ What else do you need to help you pierce through the "thick curtain of incomprehensibility" this writing may seem to be? (Dionysius on p. 32.)

Chapter Four: A Deeper Reality: Revelation 1:1–5:14

Read Revelation 1:1–5:14. Consult a Bible commentary on these passages for a brief presentation from another perspective.

Schmidt cites a passage from Jack Kerouac's *On the Road.* He uses Kerouac's writing as an example of strategies used in "oral mind" communication. Like a painter applying stroke after stroke, touching paint-laden brush to the canvas again and again, Schmidt creates for us an image of oral communication possibilities. Laying block upon block of description, Schmidt crafts a wall of comprehension upon which an image of a different way of absorbing verbal material may be projected. "You might think about it this way—now this way—then this way" (p. 48).

■ What are these strategies?
■ How do they feel to your ear? To your eye?
■ When in your life do you use "oral mind"? When "alphabet mind"?

Revisit Revelation 1:3, Schmidt's single-sentence expression of the burden of the first movement. Schmidt states, "In John's day ... words had the power to change reality. They registered a fact and the fact registered here is that the blessing has already been given" (p. 48).

■ In what ways have you experienced blessing in your own life?
■ What facts have been registered in your own time?

In discussing blessing on those who both hear and "keep" the spoken word, Schmidt asserts, "Truth is not just something given, but lived" (p. 49).

■ Cite some other examples from Scripture of "truth-that-must-be-lived."
■ Cite some examples from your own experience.
■ How does hearing and keeping the word spoken verify it?

Schmidt comments on the intimacy of the knowledge of the glorified Christ (pp. 49–51). He explores the notion of life on earth being mirrored in the councils of God. He also comments on the concepts of purity and defilement, bringing to light the enormous consequence of the choices made by the members of each congregation (p. 50).

- Compare and contrast what Schmidt describes with your own understanding of the relationship with the Divine.
- What effect does Schmidt's illumination have on your own expectations of your and God's roles together?

Schmidt articulates the crisis within the church to which John must have been responding. (See pp. 51–53.) He examines the competing perceptions that pulled at the churches. (See pp. 53–55.) Schmidt sees John's motivation to write imbedded in the question of Christian identity (p. 55).

- Consider with John's audience the radical or root issue that he will develop: *"will you live your lives according to the dictates of the culture or of Christ* (italics added, see p. 55)?"
- What impact might this dualistic question have on the kind of Christian present in a church in Asia Minor to hear John's vision read?
- What impact might this question have on the kind of Christian present to participate in a study such as this one?

Review the list of characteristics Schmidt cites identifying apocalyptic literature. (See pp. 56–57.) Review also the definition offered on page 58 as Schmidt continues his descriptive, not prescriptive task.

- What other examples of apocalyptic literature can you name from the Bible? From current literature? (Keep in mind Schmidt's suggestion that "it works well to sit lightly between the definition on the one hand and the list on the other.")
- How do you respond to Schmidt's modified definition to fit John's creative use of *apocalyptic*? (See p. 58.)

Schmidt states that influencing the behavior of people worshipping in the churches is, for John, an issue of whose spiritual authority the people recognize. Also, the "appeal to divine authority is . . . the most basic of all appeals" (p. 59).

- To what or whom do you grant authority in your own life?
- In what ways do you discern the authority of the Divine?
- How do you know when your discernment is correct?

Schmidt presents a number of images from the Hebrew Bible that John used because they were familiar to his listeners and because "[no] claim to authority for his message would have made sense without it and neither John nor his audience could have imagined a different wellspring for the images of divine rule used here" (p. 62).

- What is your own relationship with and expectation of these images?
- How do you experience the authority of "the one who . . . conquers by dying"? (See p. 62.)

Schmidt writes, "Moving, of course, from the text to our lives without co-opting Scripture to make it say what we would like for it to say—or without glossing over the considerable differences between our world and the world of the text, is the challenge" (p. 63).

- What personal habits do you have which help you meet this challenge?
- What habits are cultivated in your community to probe "the significance of Scripture for the lives of its contemporary readers" (p. 63)?

Schmidt closes this chapter with two questions that arise in a meaningful conversation with Scripture in our own day. Consider these:

- What is essential to a Christian identity shaped by the deeper reality of our lives in Christ?
- What is lost and what is gained in accommodation that we all make to the cultures around us?

Chapter Five: A Different Kind of Time: Revelation 6:1–16:21

Read Revelation 6:1–16:21. Consult a Bible commentary if you find this helpful.

Schmidt begins this chapter exploring the "power we have to shape perceptions of time and the power those perceptions have in shaping our lives" (p. 67). He comments that "the purely chronological or measurable is often of little or no relevance in [religious] literature" (p. 68).

- What are some of the various ways in which you perceive time?
- How is your sense of time different:
    when you are with children?
    during an illness?

with someone you love?

while you travel?

when you are in pain?

when you are behind schedule?

- How firmly do you hold your perception of time? Is it difficult for you to read John's "overlapping and unreconciled" (p. 69) vision with its chronological looseness?

Schmidt writes, "The expectations of God and the promised deliverance of the church reshape the religious and ethical priorities of that moment" (p. 68).

- Think of some mundane examples of changed expectations shaping the moment (e.g., the child caught with the proverbial hand in the cookie jar or an automobile accident). How does the reshaping take place?
- What experiences in your life of faith have reshaped your priorities or those of your community?
- What do you expect God to do in your life or in the future of the world?

In this chapter, Schmidt explains the seals, the trumpets, and the bowls and their probable references.

- What similarities do you find among these? What themes weave these images together?
- How do you integrate Schmidt's explanation into your understanding of Revelation?

John's vision uses images of horses and riders with messages, of mother and child, and of the dragon.

- Do some further research on how these images are used in the broader body of literature and lore.
- What echoes of meaning do these archetypes carry over from other literature to which you've been exposed?

A significant collection of specific numbers is presented in this section of John's vision.

- How do they function to support or detract from John's big-picture goal to encourage the churches while creating an acute awareness of the deeper reality in which they live?

■ How are these numbers different from the (measurements
and book pages and sizes on garment tags and time stamps
and telephones and other) numbers that surround you in
day-to-day life?

■ Why do you suppose John was so specific?

Review Schmidt's discussion of John's "horizon" and our contemporary "horizon" on pages 77–78.

■ How does your understanding of the future change the shape
of your life today?

■ How is your eschatology evolving during this study? How is
its role in your beliefs changed?

Chapter Six: A Choice of Two Cities: Revelation 17:1–22:21

Read Revelation 17:1–22:21. Consult a Bible commentary if this
is helpful.

Take a moment to absorb the story of the girl studying butterflies
and her later insight about what was missed when they were killed
and pinned to a board (pp. 79–80). Your study of Revelation hopefully has allowed you the time to "sit . . . still" and "pay attention"
with all your senses to John's vision.

■ What have you noticed?

Schmidt comments on John's decision to use cities as the central
metaphor for the choice facing the church. John is, he says, "intentionally tapping his church's memory and emotions . . . put[ting] the
choice between Christ and culture before his readers a final time,
confronting some and comforting others" (p. 81).

■ How does this image work for you today?

■ What metaphors from contemporary life might John use now?

Schmidt comments that John "both celebrates and mourns the undoing of Rome" (p. 82) as he faces the complex shape of his churches
and their pastoral demands.

■ What effects does this complexity have on the clarity of his
communication?

■ What tones of voice do you imagine John using in laying out
the case against the city? In calling out the church from the
coming plagues?

- What judgment on today's world do you both celebrate and mourn?

Revisit Schmidt's illuminations of the last seven visions on pages 83–91.
- What interpretive mistakes does Schmidt reiterate as he begins this discussion?
- Catalog the themes that John underlines again for his audience to strengthen his communication with the "oral mind."

Review the list Schmidt offers of the ways in which John brings his audience "back into the moment, [now that they have been] transformed by a vision of the realities he has revealed to them" (p. 91).
- What brings you back into focus into the moment?

Schmidt acknowledges, "Anyone who subscribes to the conviction that a person of faith must engage the world will face a choice between the cities of our own making and God's" (p. 92).
- How effective do you imagine John was in presenting the question in his own day?
- How well has John called your attention to this question in your own life?

Final Thoughts

In closing, Schmidt answers the questions he imagines you might want to ask.
- How accurate is Schmidt's guess of what you are wondering?
- How satisfactory are his answers?
- With what unanswered questions do you leave this study?
- So what?
- How are you different because of this study?
- What will you do while you wait for the One who comes?

Helen McPeak is a priest of the Diocese of Northern California. Her current manifestation as wife and mother and homemaker in Las Vegas, Nevada, will no doubt shape her future ministry.

NOTES

Introduction to the Series

1. David F. Ford, "The Bible, the World, and the Church I," in *The Official Report of the Lambeth Conference 1998* (ed. J. Mark Dyer et al.; Harrisburg, Pa.: Morehouse Publishing, 1999), 332.
2. For my broader understanding of authority, I am indebted to Eugene Kennedy and Sara C. Charles, *Authority: The Most Misunderstood Idea in America* (New York: Free Press, 1997).
3. William Sloane Coffin, *Credo* (Louisville: Westminster John Knox Press, 2003), 156.

Chapter 1: Revelation as Roadmap

1. Richard Erdoes, *A.D. 1000: A World on the Brink of Apocalypse* (Berkeley: Seastone, 1998), xi.
2. Hal Lindsey, *The Late Great Planet Earth* (Grand Rapids: Zondervan, 1970), from the back cover. Cf. Theodore Winston Pike, *Israel: Our Duty, Our Dilemma* (Oregon City, Oreg.: Big Sky Press, 1984); Grant R. Jeffrey, *Armageddon: Appointment with Destiny* (New York: Bantam Books, 1988); Charles H. Dyer, *The Rise of Babylon: Sign of the End Times* (Wheaton, Ill.: Tyndale House Publishers, Inc., 1991); Peter and Paul Lalonde, *2000 A.D.: Are You Ready? How New Technologies and Lightning-Fast Changes Are Opening the Door for Satan and His Plan for the End of the World* (Nashville: Thomas Nelson, 1997); and David Jeremiah, *Escape the Coming Night* (Dallas: Word Publishing, 2001).
3. Cathy Lynn Grossman, "Prophecy feeds fires of debate, End-of-the-world books have an eternal appeal," *USA Today*, April 22, 2004, 7D.
4. Quoted in Timothy P. Weber, *Living in the Shadow of the Second Coming* (Chicago: University of Chicago Press, 1987), 29.

5. Ibid., 29–30.
6. Lindsey, *Late Great Planet Earth*.
7. Norman Cohn, *The Pursuit of the Millennium: Revolutionary Millenarians and Mystical Anarchists of the Middle Ages* (rev. ed.; New York: Oxford University Press, 1970), 13. The italicized elements are Cohn's and the elaborations are mine.

Chapter 2: Revelation as Myth

1. R. P. C. Hanson, *Allegory and Event: A Study of the Sources and Significance of Origen's Interpretation of Scripture* (Louisville: Westminster John Knox Press, 2002), 343.
2. Eusebius, *The History of the Church from Christ to Constantine* (trans. G. A. Williamson; London: Penguin Books, 1989), 240–41 (VII.25). Emphasis mine.
3. Hugh Jackson Lawlor and John Earnest Leonard Oulton, trans., *Eusebius, Bishop of Caesarea, The Ecclesiastical History and the Martyrs of Palestine* (vol. 2; London: Society for Promoting Christian Knowledge, 1928), 102.
4. Eusebius, *The History of the Church*, 103 (III.39). See also David L. Barr, "Reading Revelation Today: Consensus and Innovations," in *Reading the Book of Revelation, A Resource for Students: Resources for Bible Study* 44 (ed. W. Ross Wagner; Atlanta: Society of Biblical Literature, 2003), 1.
5. Bruce M. Metzger, *The Canon of the New Testament: Its Origin, Development, and Significance* (Oxford: Clarendon Press, 1987), 238.
6. Ibid., 237.
7. St. Augustine, *City of God* (trans. Henry Bettenson; London: Penguin Books, 1984), 915 (20.9).
8. Jacques Ellul, *Apocalypse: The Book of Revelation* (trans. George W. Schreiner; New York: The Seabury Press, 1977).
9. See Ellul's *Presence of the Kingdom* (2nd ed.; Colorado Springs: Helmers & Howard, 1989), 56–57.
10. Ellul, *Apocalypse*, 92–93. Emphasis mine.
11. Ibid., 208.
12. Ibid., 11ff. Ellul's approach drew criticism from scholars who have studied the historical setting of John's Apocalypse. See, for example, the reviews by Elisabeth Schüssler Fiorenza in *Horizons* 5 (1978): 263f.; and Adela Yarbro Collins in *Catholic Biblical Quarterly* 40 (1978): 269f.
13. Catherine Keller, *Apocalypse Now and Then: A Feminist Guide to the End of the World* (Boston: Beacon Press, 1996), xiii.
14. Ibid., 80.
15. Ibid., 276.

Chapter 3: Revelation as History

1. Eusebius, *The History of the Church*, 240 (VII.25).
2. L. Frank Baum, *The Wonderful Wizard of Oz* (Lawrence: University Press of Kansas, 1999). The original was published by Bobbs-Merrill in 1903.

Chapter 4: A Deeper Reality: Revelation: 1:1–5:14

1. Adapted from an outline suggested by M. Eugene Boring, *Revelation: Interpretation, A Bible Commentary for Teaching and Preaching* (ed. James Luther Mays et al.; Louisville: John Knox Press, 1989), 29–30.
2. Jack Kerouac, *On the Road* (New York: Penguin Books, 1957), 307.
3. Although he does not make the connection with John's Apocalypse, I owe the comparison of Kerouac's work with Walter Ong's analysis of the oral mind to Michael Hayward at Simon Fraser University in Vancouver. See http://www.harbour.sfu.ca/~hayward/Unspeakable Visitions/Orality.html. Cf. Walter J. Ong, *Orality and Literacy: The Technologizing of the Word* (London: Routledge, 2002), 36ff.
4. Donald M. Allen and Robert Creeley, eds., *New American Story* (New York: Grove Press,1965), 270.
5. Ugo Vanni, "Liturgical Dialogue as a Literary Form in the Book of Revelation," *New Testament Studies* 37 (1991): 348ff. See also David E. Aune, *Word Biblical Commentary 52A: Revelation 1–5* (ed. Bruce Metzger; Dallas: Word Books, 1997), 11, 20.
6. Klaus Koch, *The Rediscovery of Apocalyptic* (London: SCM. Press, 1972), 24ff.
7. John J. Collins, ed., *Apocalypse: The Morphology of a Genre. Semeia* 14 (1979).
8. This is not to suggest that John's own "charismatic" authority is not an issue as well. It is. But there is no stronger way to underline that authority than to have God or Christ speak through you. See Stephen D. O'Leary, *Arguing the Apocalypse: A Theory of Millennial Rhetoric* (New York: Oxford University Press, 19974), 53f.

Chapter 5: A Different Kind of Time: Revelation: 6:1–16:21

1. Eugene Boring observes that this strategy not only helps to relieve what might otherwise lead to "sensory overload," but also to stress the point that "Christ is not the one who comes only at the end of history but the one who has already come." See Boring, *Revelation*, 99.
2. Hail and fire (Rev 8:7, cf. Exod 9:23–35); the sea of blood (Rev 8:8–9, cf. Exod 7:20); bitter water (Rev 8:10–11, cf. Exod 7:14–25); darkness (Rev

8:12, cf. Exod 10:21–23); and locusts (Rev 9:1–12, cf. Exod 10:12–20). For a useful chart see Wilfrid J. Harrington, *Revelation: Sacra Pagina* 16 (ed. Daniel J. Harrington; Collegeville: The Liturgical Press, 1993), 107. See also Boring, *Revelation*, 135.

Chapter 6: A Choice of Two Cities: Revelation: 17:1–22:21

1. Natalie B. Van Kirk, "The Difference between Catching Butterflies and the Mysteries of God" (unpublished sermon preached at the Cathedral Church of St. Matthew, Dallas, Tx., Sixth Easter: C, May 16, 2004).
2. See Boring, *Revelation*, 195ff. and Harrington, *Revelation*, 192ff. The fact that the blood on the robe of the Lamb is his own is hinted at in Rev 1:7 and is also suggested by the fact that his robe is in that condition before the battle even begins.
3. Boring, *Revelation*, 200.
4. Ibid., 215ff.
5. C. S. Lewis, *The Great Divorce* (New York: Macmillan, 1946).

The writer of Ecclesiastes could have been talking about the interest that the biblical text would generate when he wrote, "of making many books there is no end" (Eccl 12:12). So, the works cited here are no more than suggestions for further reading, selected either because of the added dimension they might lend to your appreciation of John's Apocalypse, or because they are particularly accessible guides to the issues we have been discussing.

Boesak, Allan A. *Comfort and Protest: The Apocalypse from a South African Perspective.* Philadelphia: The Westminster Press, 1987. For years a minister in the Dutch Reformed Mission Church of South Africa, Allan Boesak's introduction to the Book of Revelation draws the same kind of urgency that may well have prompted John to write the Apocalypse. As such, it is not only a reliable guide to Revelation's meaning, but serves as an important challenge to those who might otherwise miss the urgency of its message.

Boring, M. Eugene. *Revelation.* Interpretation: A Bible Commentary for Teaching and Preaching. Edited by James Luther Mays et al. Louisville: John Knox Press, 1989. Like the other books in this series, Eugene Boring's commentary was written for those who teach or preach from Scripture. It is a challenging but accessible guide to the Apocalypse and particularly valuable as a guide to the theology of the book.

Caird, G. B. *The Revelation of St. John the Divine: Black's New Testament Commentaries.* London: Adam & Charles Black, 1966. An older but still very useful commentary on John's Apocalypse,

George Caird takes the reader through a line-by-line study of the text, explaining complex issues with great clarity.

Cohn, Norman. *The Pursuit of the Millennium: Revolutionary Millenarians and Mystical Anarchists of the Middle Ages.* Rev. ed. New York: Oxford University Press, 1970. There is a great deal of literature available on the way in which people have understood and misunderstood the material in John's Apocalypse. Cohn's book provides a description that has ready application to our own day and time.

Collins, Adela Yarbro. *Crisis and Catharsis: The Power of the Apocalypse.* Philadelphia: The Westminster Press, 1984. One of the leading students of John's Apocalypse, Collins describes the historical circumstances that faced the church in Asia Minor and the role that the Book of Revelation played in helping its membership to face the challenge.

Reddish, Mitchell G. *Revelation: Smyth & Helwys Bible Commentary.* Edited by R. Scott Nash et al. Macon, Ga.: Smyth & Helwys, 2001. There are a number of longer commentaries and reference works devoted to the Book of Revelation. Reddish's work is among the more accessible and contains a number of helpful maps, diagrams, and aids.

ABOUT THE AUTHOR

The Reverend Dr. Frederick W. Schmidt Jr. is an Episcopal priest, and director of Spiritual Life and Formation and associate professor of Christian Spirituality at Southern Methodist University, Perkins School of Theology in Dallas, Texas. Canonically resident in the Diocese of Washington, he has served in numerous parishes in England and the United States, as residentiary canon of St. George's Cathedral, Jerusalem, and as canon educator at Washington National Cathedral.

A lecturer at Oxford University and tutor at Keble College, Oxford, he has also taught undergraduates in the United States, served as special assistant to the president of La Salle University in Philadelphia, Pennsylvania, and as dean of St. George's College, Jerusalem.

Dr. Schmidt holds the Doctor of Philosophy from Oxford University. His honors include a Fellowship in administrative leadership with the American Council on Education; a Senior Fellowship with the W. F. Albright Institute of Archaeological Research; and membership in Class XI of the Clergy Leadership Project. He is also a member of the Board of Examining Chaplains for the Episcopal Church, USA.

He is the author of numerous published articles and reviews, including forty-four entries in Doubleday's *Anchor Bible Dictionary*, as well as articles in *Feminist Theology, The Scottish Journal of Theology,* and *Plumbline.* He is author of *A Still Small Voice: Women, Ordination, and the Church* (Syracuse University Press, 1998), *The Changing Face of God* (Morehouse, 2000) and *When Suffering Persists* (Morehouse, 2001). He is the series editor for the new Anglican Association of Biblical Scholars Study Series.

ALSO BY FREDERICK W. SCHMIDT

When Suffering Persists:
A Theology of Candor

"Now more than ever—since the tragedy of terrorist attacks—we need this book to help us deal with the mystery of suffering in our lives."
—Sister Helen Prejean, author of *Dead Man Walking*

"At once pastoral, personal, and theological, this timely and sensitive book refuses to domesticate the mystery of our suffering with conventional explanations that blame either God or the victim, and instead affirms a relational God who is present with us in our suffering."
—Marcus Borg, author of *Reading the Bible Again for the First Time* and *Meeting Jesus Again for the First Time*

Morehouse books are available from Episcopal and online booksellers, or directly from the publisher at 800-877-0012 or online at www.morehousegroup.com.

ALSO EDITED BY FREDERICK W. SCHMIDT

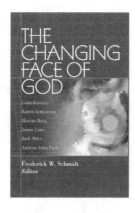

The Changing Face of God

Five leading scholars—Marcus Borg, Karen Armstrong, James Cone, Jack Miles, and Andrew Sung Park—explore why our understanding of God makes a world of difference. Excellent for parish study groups, with study questions and an introduction by the former Canon Educator of the Washington National Cathedral. Videos of the original lectures are also available from Morehouse Publishing.

"... [A]n excellent resource and a genuine guide to late twentieth-century theological questing."
—The Rev. Dr. Ronald Conner, Cathedral Age

"Readable, provocative, excellent for discussion groups."
—Washington National Cathedral

morehouse

Morehouse books are available from Episcopal and online booksellers, or directly from the publisher at 800-877-0012 or online at www.morehousegroup.com.